Recovering Connections

January 10, 1993

To Juan Lorenzo—

Who makes so
many connections.

Richard D. Grant Jr
(Nick)

Recovering Connections

Experiencing the Gospels as
Fulfilling Our Longings for
Parenting, Companionship,
Power, & Meaning

*Richard D. Grant, Jr., Ph.D.,
& Andrea Wells Miller*

HarperSanFrancisco
A Division of HarperCollinsPublishers

To Barbara and Keith

FIRST EDITION

Library of Congress Cataloging-in-Publication Data
Grant, Richard D.
Recovering connections : experiencing the Gospels as fulfilling our
longings for parenting, companionship, power, & meaning /
Richard D. Grant, Jr., Andrea Wells Miller. — 1st ed.
p. cm.
Includes bibliographical references.
ISBN 0–06–063386–7 (alk. paper)
Wells. II. Title.
BT732.5.G73 1992   248.8'6—dc20 91–70707
                                                      CIP

92 93 94 95 96 ❖ HAD 10 9 8 7 6 5 4 3 2 1
This edition is printed on acid-free paper that meets the American
National Standards Institute Z39.48 Standard.

Contents

Acknowledgments

The authors wish to thank the many people on spiritual journeys who have talked to one or the other of us about their struggle to combine their psychological healing experiences with their Christian faith.

Also, we appreciate Keith Miller's encouragement to explore the ideas that eventually led to this project. His continued support and input have been quite beneficial, both to the work itself and to our sometimes weary selves as we wrestled with the concepts.

We honed our communication of the ideas expressed here with the help of the following persons. They read an earlier draft of this work and suggested areas that they felt needed attention: Carolyn M. Bates, Barbara Budde, Michael Flahive, Howard Hovde, Carolyn Huffman, Susan Kerr, Sheila Fabricant Linn, J. Keith Miller, Jeannie O'Dell, Vicki Spencer, and Cindy Staffield. Our thanks go to each of them for this substantial gift of time. Since we did not take all of their advice, we do not hold them responsible for any errors, miscommunications, or misconceptions you may find in this book.

Beth Weber, of Harper San Francisco, gave the manuscript careful attention and made several thoughtful suggestions, for which we are very grateful. Ann tucker, the Millers' secretary, helped by accurately organizing multiple stacks of manuscripts, making the process of mining the helpful comments from our readers a much easier task.

Working with all these people has benefited this project immensely and has enriched our lives as we continue to strive to make connections among various sorts of information about spiritual and psychological healing.

Richard D. Grant, Ph.D.   Andrea Wells Miller
Austin, Texas   Austin, Texas

Introduction

It was a cold, dark Wednesday night in February, and I was tired. My husband, Keith, and I had just moved to Austin, Texas, from a little town on the Gulf Coast, and I was overwhelmed by the increased traffic and general complexity of living in the capital city of Texas. He and I were sitting in the parish hall of St. Matthew's Episcopal Church watching members of the congregation lazily moving through supper cleanup to evening speaker, a local psychologist giving the first of a series of talks during Lent, the six weeks before Easter. The noisy clatter of folding chairs on the tile floor intensified my headache, and a sea of strange faces chattered and smiled at each other and at me. I felt grim and impatient. The next forty-five minutes loomed endlessly ahead like the last day of school for a child. I was too worn out and dazed by the strangeness of town, home, and people to do anything more than endure the rest of the evening.

Spiritual Pain Comes Even to Christians

The night before, I had written in my journal about the split I felt within me. There seemed to be a missing link between my psychological recovery experiences and my involvement with Christianity.

I knew my Christian path needed to include Bible study, attending church, tithing, prayer, and reaching out to others, but I was struggling to make these activities meaningful and healing for my wounded soul—both the inner child and the adult woman. I could only dimly glimpse the connections between psychological and emotional health and spiritual growth, and I had trouble finding the connection with specific Christian principles. I was born into a Christian family, raised in the church, and gave my life to Jesus at age nine. Yet I still wound up as confused, pain-filled, and shame-based as many people I had met who had not had such a childhood. I felt cut off from a personal relationship with God, even though I knew such a relationship was necessary for fulfillment. What had gone wrong?

I had experienced much improvement through therapy, Twelve-Step groups, reading, and journaling. I felt a rekindled desire for a meaningful personal relationship with God. But I simply didn't know quite how to bring my spiritual wounds, pain, and longing to God.

A New Window Opened

That evening, I continued to fret over this dilemma, and I fully expected the speaker to be off base as far as my own spiritual struggle was concerned, because up until then, with a few exceptions, most Christian speakers had been. Then the speaker, Dr. Richard D. Grant, Jr., approached the podium and began to talk.

With an incisive sense of humor, sound sources that supported his opinions, and a strong and reverent faith, he presented the Gospel of Matthew in a way I will never forget, and he promised in the coming weeks to walk with us into Mark, Luke, and John. He spoke to the spiritual longing I had to reconnect to God in a personal way that took into account my individuality, my life's experiences, and my present, everyday situation. His fresh way of thinking, engaging speaking style, and spiritual groundedness opened a new window through which I could see more clearly a way to become more open to God.

My fatigue evaporated. My husband and I waited in line until we could talk to Nick (as Dr. Grant is known). Keith asked, "Have you ever considered writing a book about these things?"

Nick flashed a shy grin and raised his eyebrows. "Yes," he said, "I've tried. But I can't seem to get anywhere."

I chimed in, "Maybe we should talk. I like to write for people who don't like writing, don't have time to do it, or don't write for whatever reason." And that night, over five years ago, Richard Grant and I began the dialogue that resulted in this book.

In our first meeting, Nick said that this material had him—he didn't have it. He hadn't had a clear idea of what to do with the material beyond speaking about it, and he was pleased that an experienced writer like Keith Miller thought the material would be helpful as a book. When he heard my invitation to talk about writing together, he told me he was surprised to learn that I write from people's lectures. As I listened to him, I gradually began to see that I had a legitimate role to play that would not only make this healing material available to others but also allow me to explore *for myself* the healing links between therapy and faith, between my wounded soul and Jesus Christ, my Lord and Savior.

Our Beliefs May Bar the Door to Spiritual Growth

I had been told that our knowledge and beliefs about God come to us from less-than-perfect people in our family and church—and that we get a lot of it wrong either because of the way people taught us or because of our immature perception of what they told us.

Perhaps we see God as harsh and intimidating, or as waiting for us to foul up in order to punish us with lightning-bolt intensity. Or possibly we see God as one who exists to do our will—sort of a Holy Genie who is to meet our needs or grant our wishes whenever we ask for anything, so that we feel hurt or angry when our prayers "don't work." Or maybe God seems to be loving yet busy with things more important than us, before whom we must stand in line—and there is a long, long line—leaving us with little hope of personal connection. Or perhaps God is seen as one who dispenses love and approval only as we earn it through perfect behavior or performance of some kind.

Those of us who have had such images stored in our hearts may not realize that we have made God in the image of our imperfect care givers—parents, teachers, ministers, and others. We are not clear about who God is and what God wants to do for us. So we may turn elsewhere, believing, or at least hoping, that something else will bring us the sense of security, connection, power, and wisdom we need.

On finding that certain paths haven't helped our pain or brought us security and serenity, many of us turn to counselors, treatment centers, Twelve-Step groups, or a combination of these. Almost all of these point to a spiritual aspect of living that is vital to our recovery. However, as long as our distorted beliefs about God remain in our minds, we are cut off from the very security, solace, and strength we need in order to come to wholeness and freedom in recovery. And yet beyond all reasonable expectations God continues to seek us out.

Renovating Distorted Beliefs

During these past few years, it has become increasingly clear that renovating our distorted beliefs and establishing a nurturing, healthy relationship with a deeply caring, all-powerful, trustworthy, nonabusive God can be as simple (though not easy) as turning around in the midst of our pain, ceasing to seek satisfaction for our profound longings from inappropriate sources, and opening our minds to the possibility that our beliefs need to be adjusted. As we consciously seek intimate contact with God in this new turning to God, we begin to experience God's true and loving nature. It has been a welcome relief to discover at a whole different level that the more I open my mind and heart on my side of the relationship, the more God can teach me who God is, reveal to me what is best for my life, and show me the path to security, healthy relationships, and appropriate power and meaning for my life.

Weaving Old Ideas Together Leads to a Fresh Look at Truth

The ideas that we present in this book are like the strands of straw in a basket. Each strand by itself is a valid unit. When several strands are woven together, they create a container that has more strength than the individual strands by themselves. The strands we have woven together include elements of depth psychology, childhood development theory, the effect of childhood wounds on adults, and the direct healing role of Jesus Christ in our lives as described in the four Gospels and specifically in some of the parables of Jesus.

Although some of the connections we have discovered and described may seem complex, we have worked to make them as simple and clear as we could. We explore each strand and then weave them together with other strands into a finished basket that embodies the spiritual roots of childhood wounds and the experience of spiritual healing for these root wounds. By taking the time to explore each strand, you may discover a way to weave for yourself a "basket" that will hold together your God-given personality and the various parts of your study, life experience, intuitive understanding, and prayer life—the tools with which you can cultivate an inner life that leads to experiences of spiritual healing.

Working with each strand and seeing how the strands fit together has given me a new way of seeing the healing message of Christ. I have begun to integrate therapy and faith and find much spiritual healing in this process of redirecting my wounded, unsatisfied, longing soul toward God. I have seen in the Bible and in my experience that there *is* a satisfying milieu in which the inner longings for parenting, companionship, power, and meaning can find their creative resolution—and in a certain kind of relationship to God, their fulfillment.

Enter an Adventure Toward Spiritual Wholeness!

I invite you to take a look with Nick and me at this blend of psychological truths, Christian traditions, and biblical study, in search of your own approach to recovering connections with God.

Andrea Wells Miller
Austin, Texas

Part I

Spiritual Wounds

I

The Spiritual Root of Addiction and Codependence

It is widely accepted that growing up in a dysfunctional family contributes heavily to adult codependence and addictions. But another factor may also contribute to the creation of this painful condition—a spiritual factor.

How God Makes Contact with the Human Soul

We have within us from birth the capacity for experiencing profound internal energies. Certain events in our lives trigger the release of these energies that John of the Cross called "urgent longings."[1] They have also been called primordial energies, destiny, angelic messages, spiritual power, and being moved by something bigger than oneself. C. G. Jung refers to these capacities for experiencing internal energies as *archetypes*.[2] They are evidently universal spiritual points of contact with God, who created the psyche, or soul,[3] of human beings.

The word *archetype* is much more than a psychological term. One of its earliest recorded uses was by a second-century A.D. Christian bishop named Iraneus (I-ra-nay'-us), in describing how God's action made contact with the soul.[4] Because *arche* means beginning or origin, and *typos* means impression, the full word literally means "original impression." Another early Christian writer, Dionysius, compared an archetype to a metal signet ring making a stamp in different materials, such as clay, metal, and wood. The shape of the stamp on the signet ring is the same, but because the materials are different, there are individual differences in how the stamp impression looks.[5] In the same way, when certain events take place, people respond in strikingly similar ways, with a set of emotions, thoughts, and behaviors designed to insure survival and meet needs. But like the distinctive impression left by the signet ring, people's expressions of these responses are individual. For example, when expressing fear or shock, some people laugh nervously, some hide, some freeze, some attack. Falling in love has a general form, but the exact experience of a particular couple is unique. In the same way, when a child says "Goo" and smiles, parents experience a tremendous feeling of care giving—the bonding experience—but the exact parenting behavior of a particular mother or father is expressed individually.

The Purpose of Archetypes

If we human beings encounter a situation that provides the right stimulation, a corresponding archetype, or "contact point," is triggered, releasing energies in a pattern individually suited to that situation. These energies are activated by two elements interacting: an *encounter with certain situations*, usually a dilemma or crisis where we need to draw on deep inborn responses to help us adapt; and *developmental stages in life* in which it is appropriate for us to be working through certain life experiences. We most often experience the activation of these energies in one of these ways: (1) when our conscious efforts to solve a problem are frustrated and we don't have a solution, (2) when we experience a contradiction and the way we've ordinarily behaved doesn't resolve it anymore, or (3) when we encounter a person or situation that has a profound, disturbing impact on us.

Contact points, when activated, provide us with energy, information, and inborn responses to the information. It's as if God provides us with an internal survival kit full of things we will need to confront various life experiences and not only survive, but thrive, nurtured by a divinely inspired plan of existence. Today various groups call such thriving by a variety of names: recovery, living in process, going with the flow, walking in God's will, experiencing psychological health, being saved, being functional.

Energy: The energy pattern is like a riverbed that isn't seen as a riverbed until water rushes into it and suddenly there's a stream. It is like an entire set of subroutines on a microchip, waiting for the proper command to activate the appropriate subroutine. Within a person, such energy might be described as the hunger in our heart for the object of our ultimate longings. This hunger draws us to God as the satisfier of these longings.

Information: Like "psychic organs," activated contact points are designed to give us information from our psychological experiences, just as our physical organs, eyes, ears, noses, and the senses of touch and taste give us information from the physical world. These psychic organs are the basic framework within which we experience psychological reality. The energy pattern thus released not only helps us become *aware* of our experience and gives us energy for dealing with it, it also gives us a way to *embody, organize, and make some sense* of it.

Inborn Responses: Interesting studies of infants by Spitzer and of animals by Lorenz suggest how contact points and their energy patterns might operate within human beings. Lorenz both points to behaviors such as a wren nesting or a wasp stinging a caterpillar in just the right place to incapacitate it. Animals know what to do and when to do it to survive. In a similar way, a baby's smile or cry rivets adult attention and care giving onto the child, which is essential for its survival.

The released energies "tell" us what to do. They enable us to prioritize our behavior and "do the right thing." For example, a person falling in love somehow knows what to do as a lover, much like lovers throughout the centuries have done.

How We Know a Contact Point Has Been Triggered

It is helpful to know the distinction between a contact point itself and the image it produces. The contact point is unknowable, completely unconscious, extremely vigorous, leading to certain individual and cultural expressions. It is an energy point deep within the soul. For it to become known and understood, it first needs to be projected on to some appropriate external experience, the way an image is projected onto a movie screen. We recognize the energy pattern of a contact point by its image embodied in a real-life situation.

When we experience a triggering event, the tremendous energy released from that place deep within our unconscious mind, or psyche, is "projected" onto the external event or experience, serving as a screen for us to see. Even if a dream triggers a contact point, the dream seems to have more impact than other dreams, with power, clarity, and a compelling quality to it that is different from an ordinary dream. Such a dream can use images from our daily lives or ones that are completely different from our daily experience.

Two distinguishing qualities accompany the triggering of a contact point:

We feel tremendous emotional intensity that has great impact on us as a result of the triggering encounter. For example, a woman, whom we'll call Nicole, once dreamed that an eagle landed on her shoulder and she felt the enormous power of the eagle's beak grasping her index finger. When she awoke, she easily remembered the dream. Nicole had been toying with ideas for a play for some time, and made the connection between the imagery and her sense of being called to write. Her dream offered a sustaining image to support her in pursuing the writing. The imagery certainly came from outside her daily experience—an eagle had never landed on her shoulder. This extraordinary image and its emotional intensity reveal it as an *archetypal* dream—one that triggered a contact point, releasing an energy pattern within the dreamer.

Robert Johnson says that when we've had a nightmare, we should pay attention to it because through the dream God is tapping a foot, and saying, in effect, "Wake up! Pay attention to this area of your life before it is too late!"

We first perceive the emotional intensity to be somehow related to an external stimulus—someone or something outside ourselves—rather than a psychological part of ourselves. For example, Bonnie, a happily married woman in her late thirties, noticed that on recent visits to her doctor, she experienced a strong attraction toward him. At first she perceived it as a sexual fascination for the man himself—an object outside herself. But as Bonnie wrestled with the implications of these strong feelings, she eventually identified her *own* attraction to the field of medicine, a part of her own developmental journey.

The emotional intensity accompanying the activation of a contact point feels like the "urgent longings" described by John of the Cross. Nicole realized her longing to write a play; Bonnie identified her longing to be a doctor.

Communication with God

A relationship seems to exist between the energy pattern of contact points and God's messengers—angels. In most Judaic and Christian theologies, angels serve as "intermediary realities" that convey the will of God to humanity. Thomas Aquinas, one of the greatest scholars regarding angels, said that angels communicate with people, first by creating a fantasy image in their minds, then by empowering the intellect to understand it. This is another way of describing a contact point. A dream can contain archetypal images that convey a powerful message ("angel" = "messenger") to our conscious life. This suggests a strong connection between the biblical concept of angels and what Jung meant by archetypes. Perhaps when we talk about archetypes we're really talking about God's messengers as well.

For example, in the New Testament, an angel told Joseph in a dream to get up, take the child Jesus and his mother, and flee to the land of Egypt (Matt. 2:13). Imagine Joseph experiencing tremendous emotional intensity, waking up in a cold sweat, and thinking, "They're going to kill this child." The dream has so much impact that Joseph is gripped by a compelling realization with a quality of illumination and profound truth and urgency—he'd *better* do something about it. The images and words of Joseph's dream activated a paternal care-giving energy that was so strong and focused that Joseph acted immediately to save the child's life.

The Spiritual Root of Addiction and Codependence

When our first encounters with contact points occur within a dysfunctional family, the energy, information, and inborn responses from our internal survival kit are often misdirected and distorted in the way we respond to others. We may reach adulthood without healthy fulfillment of the deep, profound yearnings that are triggered. The spiritual factor that sets up codependence and addictions can be seen in this process. Not only do the painful experiences that come from *outside ourselves* set up codependence and addictions, the profound force of the activated contact point *within ourselves* drives us into the painful experience. The *combined* result of both the outside painful experience and the internal driving force brings us the sense of incompleteness and inadequacy characterizing codependence, an internal pain that many people may learn to alleviate, temporarily, with an addictive process.

When the addictive process no longer works as a pain reliever, we may decide to intervene and break our addiction. We then turn to more beneficial and appropriate things to find healing and set these wrongs right. Perhaps we enter therapy and resolve our emotional scars from the traumas of the past. We may practice behavior modification techniques and develop practical skills in living and relating. These may alleviate much of the pain of codependence and help us stay free of our addictions. But it seems that if we do not address these powerful internal longings and develop our spiritual capacity for connection with God, we are likely to experience recurrences of the pain of codependence to varying degrees, and perhaps even begin a new addiction or experience relapses into our previous ones.

As long as these spiritual contact points continue to be misdirected, distorted, or denied, it seems that we are likely to be thwarted in the ability to care for ourselves with respect and deal with our emotions, thinking, and behavior in ways that enrich our lives. We may still be impaired in our ability to form healthy relationships with ourselves, with others, and with God. Without appropriate activation and guidance, our internal survival kit seems to malfunction just when we need it most.

Appropriate connection to God through the development of our spiritual capacities gives us the greatest opportunity to break free from these self-defeating ways of experiencing life into optimum recovery—truly thriving as God meant us to live. Many people with addictions and codependence turn to the effective recovery process of the Twelve-Step program developed by Alcoholics Anonymous. One of the suggestions made in those steps entails developing and continuing to practice "conscious contact with God."

The Big Book of Alcoholics Anonymous makes certain promises "to those who thoroughly follow our path" (the Twelve Steps). Two of these promises are that we will "intuitively know how to handle situations which used to baffle us," and "not regret the past nor wish to shut the door on it."[6] These two promises speak of healing in the areas of distorted and misdirected energy patterns. When we intuitively know how to handle baffling situations, our internal survival kit is able to deliver the energy, information, and inborn responses that the contact points provide. When we no longer regret the past, we have come to terms with the painful experiences of our lives, and have acknowledged that our pain brought us back into proper contact with a loving, supportive, healing God.

By looking more deeply at how improper expressions of certain basic contact points may have contributed to our codependence and addictions, we can deepen our recovery experience by redirecting the energies provided by each contact point, thus moving ourselves toward more appropriate contact with God.

NOTES

1. St. John of the Cross, "The Dark Night," *Collected Works*, trans. Kivan Kaugnaught and Otilio Rodriguez (Washington, DC: Institute of Carmelite Studies Publications, 1973), p. 295.
2. C. G. Jung, Collected Works No. 9, *The Archetypes and the Collective Unconscious* (Princeton: Bollinger, 1968).
3. Morton Kelsey, *Myth, History, and Faith* (Rockport: Element Press, 1974).
4. Jolande Jacobi, "Archetype," in Bollingen Series LVII, *Complex, Archetype, Symbol* (New York: Princeton Univ. Press, 1959), p. 34: The term [archetype] . . . occurs in Iraneus: "the creator of the world did not fashion these things directly from himself, but copied them from archetypes outside himself." (From A*dversus haereses*, II, 7, 5.)
5. Jolande Jacobi, p. 34: The term 'archetype', introduced in 1919 and today in general use, was taken by Jung from the *Corpus Hermeticum* (God is "the archetypal light") and from Dionysius, the Areopagite: "that the seal is not entire and the same in all its impressions . . . is not due to the seal itself, . . . but the difference

of the substances which share it makes the impressions of the one, entire, identical archetype to be different." (From Dionysius, *On the Divine Names* [translator C. E. Rolt], pp. 72, 62.)

6. *Alcoholics Anonymous* (New York: Alcoholics Anonymous World Services, Inc., 1976), pp. 83–84.

2

Four Contact Points in Our Soul

Many adult children of alcoholics (or of otherwise dysfunctional people) can identify the "ideal" or "functional" parental behavior that would have nurtured them even though they may have seen few examples of such functional adult behavior. Many adults can identify within themselves a deep longing to be in a satisfying romantic relationship with someone even if they have not had one. Many people living life from a victim stance can nevertheless imagine a nonabusive, self-sustaining, and dignified way to live. And many people are haunted by an awareness that there is a meaning and purpose to the various events in their lives that they have not yet discovered. In fact, almost all of us experience these four longings at various times. They can be described as the foundation of the psyche.

Many contact points (archetypes) and their corresponding deep longings have been identified and explored by writers such as C. G. Jung,[1] Anthony Stevens,[2] Carol Pearson,[3] and others. But four particular longings seem to be strongly associated with the symptoms of codependence described by Pia Mellody, Terry Kellogg, John Bradshaw, and others. They are:

1. the deep longing for parenting,
2. the deep longing for companionship and emotional development,
3. the deep longing for power and freedom, and
4. the deep longing for meaning and purpose.[4]

Deep Longing for Parenting

When a child is first held by its care givers, the child has a profound encounter with that care giver.[5] This encounter activates the child's archetypal image of the kind of perfect parent that would meet his or her needs. A complete range of responses becomes available to the child so that he or she can attract the parent to take care of him or her.

For example, research demonstrates that the smile reflex in babies occurs in response to a human face. Researchers presented to babies various combinations of facial features, such as a face with the eyes below the nose, to find just the arrangement that would elicit the baby's smile, and babies seem to be programmed to smile when presented with a close proximity of a human face.[6] Smiling behavior is, we believe, the result of the energy pattern's activation helping the baby to behave in a way that attracts the care givers. In most cases this creates a loop between the child and adult. The adult feels a personal response from the baby—many smiles aren't just from gas pain—and this enhances the bonding process. Thus, the emotional response in the care giver activates the child's psychological resources for getting what the child needs—physical care, physical nurture, emotional nurture, and so on. Spitzer's studies show that in many cases of profound neglect where the parents disappear (die or otherwise abandon the child), the baby, kept in a crib in an institution and not picked up, held, and so forth, will die. Relying on a care giver is *vital for survival,* and an inner contact point energizes the child to do his or her part in moving toward the care giver to get that need met by sending out effective signals.

Here is a further example of the reality of this contact point. People come to counseling wondering whether or not they got enough nurturing from their parents, and some feel they didn't. They make comments such as, "I wish Mom or Dad had been more supportive of me, held me more," and so on. Despite the fact that these people didn't receive perfect parenting they are able to compare the parenting they received with some internal point of reference, namely the deep inner image that was activated when they first encountered their parents.

Deep Longing for Companionship and Emotional Development

The contact point and its energy, associated with our deep longing for companionship and emotional development, involves the lifelong experience of finding friends, falling in love, or connecting with a soul mate. This experience begins in childhood when a child first interacts independently with other people, especially family.

For example, as adults, many of us expect a sexual relationship to provide complete personal fulfillment and connection. Our undistorted inner image is of a lifetime spent with another, who complements us and brings us joy. We believe such a relationship is possible even though we may never have experienced it or seen it at close range. We seem to have an inner point of reference or image for this. Where does that image come from? We believe its source is in this specific contact point and its energy pattern, "describing for us the companionship and emotional development we long for."

This contact point and its energy pattern meet our needs to adapt to life in two ways. First, the drive for companionship unites people in fruitful relationships of all kinds: biological, cultural, artistic, spiritual, and so on. Second, the drive provides personal growth for each participant in the relationship. We grow through relationship with others and through dealing with their response to us. Therefore it is important for our growth that we find a healthy tension between the need for being a separate individual and the need for intimacy. We develop boundaries and a sense of independent self by seeing ourselves mirrored in the responses of others toward us. It is virtually impossible to develop an independent sense of self without relating to others.

There are many myths describing this deep inner image for companionship, such as tales of heroes or heroines journeying and meeting companions along the way, or of two lovers struggling to be with each other. The heroes' stories tell of adventures and deeds accomplished with others. There may be different companions for different parts of the journey. The lovers' story is one of intense feelings generated in both partners, leading them to extraordinary discoveries and actions. Both types of stories show the archetypal energy that is released and experienced as intense emotionality when a friendship or love relationship is formed.

Different companions can relate to different aspects each person possesses, bringing them out for development, and accompanying the person on his or her journey. Perhaps one's spouse or significant other relates to many of one's aspects, but not all. Hence, we may yearn for other friends, even if we are experiencing fulfillment in those areas where a spouse or special person relates.

We develop as human beings by relating to each of the people to whom we are connected. These connections are a permanent part of our emotional history. Although our involvement may not be lifelong, it is still necessary and enriching. The treasure we receive from having known and loved each person seems to be the kind of treasure the Bible refers to, "treasure the thief cannot break in and steal nor the moth destroy" (Matt. 6:20). Through such relationships we grow spiritually.

When a particular energy pattern is activated, we are strongly attracted to an individual, either in a friendship or a romantic relationship. At midlife, men often go through an intimacy crisis, while women may experience an identity crisis.

Men and women struggle with both issues, of course; however, at midlife there seems to be a difference in emphasis according to gender.[7] For each, it is helpful to be aware that a strong attraction to another person most likely includes a message about an area of personal growth.

Intimacy crisis: A man may experience a sexual attraction for someone that seems inappropriate. Encountering this inner sexual connection and image can often mean the beginning of a time of emotional growth. The person to whom the man is attracted may be someone at work, where men and women often spend quality time together that sometimes amounts to more quality time than they have with their spouses or significant others. Another way this intimacy crisis happens can be when a man begins to feel disillusioned, discouraged, or angry in his marriage or primary commitment. He becomes sexually sensitive to other potential romantic partners, and begins scanning the surroundings for them. For a while, he doesn't feel he has actually "fallen in love" with someone specific, but then he may meet a particular person and project onto that person the potential and promise of his own emotional development. The person seems to offer him all the happiness that he does not experience with his family and spouse.

When this happens, he may wonder, "Do I just 'sit on it' and sweat?" Or "Am I a terrible person because I am feeling this way, even though I am already in a committed relationship?" Actually at this point he may be separating at last from his mother and, without realizing it, projecting his need to separate from his mother on the "local representative," his wife. At midlife, it is essential for many men to leave a woman. But they need to leave the right one.

Identity crisis: For women at midlife this connecting point and its energy seem to operate a little differently, and be experienced as an identity crisis. The identity crisis seems to be fueled more by the deep inner longing for power and freedom, to be discussed later in this chapter.

Finding the direction of spiritual development: If we realize that these crises may contain messages to ourselves about our internal growth, we can interact with the *inner image* coming from our activated contact point and channel the energy of this inner dynamic where it belongs—to spiritual/psychological development.

When we begin to deal with this inner image, the external attraction usually will diminish. A man, for example, may still be sensitive to the attractive woman, but will recognize that she is not someone with whom to have an affair, but rather the appropriate screen onto which he might project an inner image with its information and specific energy regarding a character in his internal history.

Having dealt with the inner image, he can move beyond the sheer strength of the attraction to consider other factors, for example whether he is free to engage in a romantic relationship or committed to stay in a previously established relationship, or whether the person's other attributes (besides romantic or sexual ones) are compatible enough with his.

We begin by distinguishing between the attractive inner image and the human being onto whom it is being projected. Writing down the attractive qualities of people (or the person) who interest us helps us discover the inner image and its message. These qualities are often metaphors about ourselves and our own development needs. For example, a daring woman willing to "risk discovery" to have an affair might represent a part of the man longing to break loose and start his own business. Next, writing a history of all the people to whom we have been attracted can help us become aware of our emotional growth history as reflected in our romantic attractions across our lifetime.

Distinguishing between the energy that is meant for self-development and the sexual attraction for a person is a safeguard against being swept away by the external issue and losing our balanced perspective. Through this distinction, we can gain a clearer sense about what to pursue for our personal spiritual/ psychological development and what to do about the attraction to the other person.

Deep Longing for Power and Freedom

The deep inner drive for power and freedom (power in action) is first encountered in childhood as the child begins to take the initiative in relationships, trying to get needs met in a more active, even confrontational way.

In adulthood, this energy might be activated again in a person who up until now has not seemed to be very courageous. Sent somewhere by the army, for example, a man finds himself fighting against people he believes to be truly oppressive and evil. He exhibits very brave behavior; he has put on the uniform, and now he's a warrior, a fighting person. "Battle fury" as seen in the military heroes of ancient Israel was considered to be one of the signs of God's presence, an activated energy pattern, as in the story of Samson (Judges 15:14–16).

We see again the energy from this contact point when someone jumps into a raging river and rescues a drowning person, when a mother lifts a car off her child, or when a person in an oppressive situation suddenly just won't take it anymore, and the sense of outrage is so strong that he or she has the energy to do something about it, even in the face of great personal danger. This energy can give us the strength to look at ourselves courageously, as a person in a Twelve-Step program does when working the Fourth Step. (See Appendix A for all twelve Steps.) We have great need of the energy from this contact point to confront one of our strongest adversaries: our own denial.

Another example of this longing for power energy is the admonishing or confronting of someone who's doing something wrong. In some situations, a person may know that if he or she confronts someone the struggle is going to be a long haul, and that he or she is vulnerable to losing something. He or she faces the issue of fortitude—really having the courage of one's convictions when there is a price to pay. And the person might realize in a moment of truth, "Well, I'm willing to sacrifice that," and perform the courageous act anyway. In that one moment, the person is brave. Others say, "Wow, Brooke was brave," and she thinks, "That wasn't brave. I just did what I had to do." It may even feel embarrassing to have this big hoopla about how brave she is. Rather than feeling brave, Brooke has a sense that a force almost greater than her conscious will was helping her, the energy pattern released by her encounter with the person or situation.

People tend to get excited when they witness such "heroic" behavior because those who know what the person is normally like find the contrast impressive. Every person has an inner warrior that can be activated given the right circumstances.[8, 9]

The midlife identity crisis that some women experience is another signal of this energy's activation. A woman may become deeply aware of a need for objective accomplishment, recognition, financial reward, or involvement in the larger world. Rather than being identified as a support staff defined by relationship to others (Bobby and Sally's mother, Fred's wife), she may long for an independent identity. She may become strongly fascinated by an idea, a career, a cause, or an institution. She may become so compelled by the truth of something that she even contemplates beginning a movement, and she feels tremendous energy to do this.

If she realizes that this fascination may include a message to her about her own inner dynamic, she can write out the attributes of the idea, cause, career, or institution that so attract and fulfill her. As in the previous discussion of a sexual attraction, distinguishing between the energy that is meant for her self-development and the energy that should be directed outward helps keep her from being swept away by the strength of the outer attraction and avoiding the inner developmental task. Since many attributes of the idea or career will be a matter of personal growth, they need to be examined and confronted first in her inner life. Then she is more likely to be able to make a decision about what to do with the idea, cause, career, or institution from a balanced perspective.

The issue of power and freedom is at the core of this contact point and its energy. The person experiencing it in a functional way knows what to do and has a sense of timing: it's not a time to speak, it's a time to do.

Deep Longing for Meaning and Purpose

This contact point and its energy are first encountered in childhood whenever some familiar circumstance of life is changed, and the child has to come to grips with a new situation. For example, when Jenny's parents moved across town, Jenny was confronted with a host of new circumstances: the arrangement of rooms inside the new house (even finding the bathroom in the night was a new experience), a new neighborhood with new children in it, a new school, and so on. The experience activated her drive for meaning, for finding out how to get along in this new environment. Supported by her parents, teachers, and others, and strengthened by the energy release, she is able to transfer a sense of organization and meaning from one environment to another.

In adults, the deep longing for meaning and purpose is reactivated at other times. It is perhaps best illustrated by the need to be in contact with a Higher Power as exemplified by the major religions of humanity and in the Third, Sixth, Seventh, and Eleventh Steps of the Twelve Steps. (See Appendix A for the Twelve Steps.)

Viktor Frankl based a form of psychotherapy called logotherapy entirely on meaning. He suggested people who have no meaning in life get sick with what he calls *nöogenic* (lack-of-meaning) *neurosis*.[10] He based this theory on his experience in Auschwitz, where people who lost their sense of personal meaning, who had nothing to live for, just died. He could look in their eyes and tell whether or not they would die. He said that one was reduced to naked existence in the concentration camp, and day by day one had to find a reason to live. Frankl himself lived because he got a sense of personal meaning from envisioning the book he was going to write.

This contact point and its energy impels people to develop scientific theories and explanatory systems and conceptual matrices of things. We may become willing to go back and look at our families of origin and plow through all the memories and events to make sense of them, to get our history straight, and to search for truth. This inner energy pattern electrifies us to search for a point of perspective, a psychological lever, that we can use to find meaning.

Other occasions that might trigger this contact point include going to a foreign country, getting into a relationship that turns you upside down, going to college, losing your job, having major surgery, or having a door shut in your face through which you always thought you were supposed to go.

In life experiences, we encounter paradoxes in which the thing we thought we were supposed to do doesn't work out and we must sit back and ask ourselves, "Now what am I supposed to do?" As this happens, the contact point and its energy pattern are often activated.

For example, Dan had his heart set on being a pilot and he became one. But soon afterward Dan developed tachycardia and was physically disqualified. Everything in Dan screamed, "I'm a pilot, pilot, pilot," but now he can no longer be a pilot. A crisis such as this triggers the release of energy from this inner contact point. Some kind of new synthesis must occur, fueled by the energy of this contact point, so that something else can give Dan a reason to live, a sense of meaning for his life.[11] Dan may become motivated to be an aircraft designer, a writer of stories about pilots, or something totally unrelated to flying.

Jesus frequently created paradox in his parables, posing a dilemma so the people listening would either be boggled by the contradiction and reject the story, or be taken to a whole new level of ethical meaning and truth. The way Jesus talked to people triggered this energy pattern within them, and it can do so for us today.

NOTES

1. Jolanda Jacobi, Bollinger Series LVII, *Complex, Archetype, Symbol in the Psychology of C. G. Jung* (New York: Princeton Univ. Press, 1971).
2. Anthony Stevens, *Archetypes* (New York: Quill Press, 1982).
3. Carol Pearson, *The Hero Within* (San Francisco: Harper San Francisco, 1985).
4. For further explanation of these four archetypes, see Edward C. Whitmont, chapter 11, *The Symbolic Quest* (Princeton: Princeton Univ. Press, 1978) and Tad Guzie and Noreen Guzie, *About Men and Women* (New York: Paulist Press, 1986).
5. It is to the *child's* archetypal encounter with the parent, not the parent's archetypal encounter, that we are referring. Incidentally, the child's experience is echoed in the parent as he or she reflects the joy of the child because the parent has a memory of the joy of being held as a child.
6. Anthony Stevens, *Archetypes* (New York: Quill Press, 1983), p. 57.
7. For more about the observation that men and women seem to face midlife crises with different emphases, see Carol Pearson, *Awakening the Hero Within* (San Francisco: Harper San Francisco, 1991), pp. 99–100.

8. See Richard D. Grant, Jr., chapter 2, "The Hero's Journey and the Twelve Steps" in *Symbols of Recovery: The Twelve Steps at Work in the Unconscious* (Philadelphia: Type and Temperament Press, Inc., 1990).

9. See Carol Pearson, chapter 8, "The Warrior" in *Awakening the Heroes Within* (San Francisco: Harper San Francisco, 1991).

10. Viktor Frankl, *Man's Search for Meaning* (New York: Beacon Press, 1963).

11. See Carol Pearson, chapter 15, "The Magician" in *The Hero Within* (San Francisco: Harper San Francisco, 1991).

3

God's Hidden Contact Points in Action

In an ideal world, a child is born into a supportive, nurturing family. The child thrives, and his or her body, mind, emotions, and soul unfold like a flower. The resulting adult is mature and well-balanced, being capable of loving and being loved, thinking and learning, feeling a full range of emotions, taking responsibility for his or her own needs and wants, and sharing himself or herself appropriately with other well-balanced mature people.

From birth, we experience growth and progress along a path that has been examined from assorted theories and vantage points. Psychologists tell us we are born with natural characteristics and inborn potentials that come into play as we evolve toward adulthood. Along the way we pass through various psychological stages, we negotiate developmental tasks, and we experience the activation of several contact points and their energies. When all goes according to plan, we journey through a magnificent array of experiences designed by our Creator to generate men and women who can live up to our potentials, accept and deal with our imperfections (or immaturity) and unexpected changes and circumstances in a constructive, positive way, and develop a capacity to be in close contact with this Creator and so discover the purpose God has for our life.

Natural Characteristics of a Child

We have already explored the inborn potentials God implants in each of us, which we described as contact points containing energy patterns. In addition, children are born with certain natural characteristics that come into play as a child matures and develops. Pia Mellody has given us a wonderful picture of five of these characteristics in her book *Facing Codependence:* preciousness (value), neediness and dependence, vulnerability, imperfection, and immaturity.[1] These characteristics are clearly also "archetypal," evidence of God's deep imprinting of potential energies within each person. The characteristics point to and are colored by each of the four energy patterns we have just discussed:

- A child's preciousness or sense of value is an overall characteristic that includes all the other characteristics and when present shields him or her like an umbrella.
- A child's neediness and dependence is the deep urge to connect with the perfect parent.
- A child's vulnerability is connected to the strong yearning for a soul mate, companionship of a deep and satisfying nature, and emotional growth and development.
- A child's imperfection is played out in trial-and-error learning and the increase of individual power leading to effectiveness or competence in the world. We do things incorrectly, experience the consequences, then correct ourselves as we continuously explore and experiment with our environment.
- A child's immaturity leads the child to learn to experience the particular reality of his or her age level. This is the personal framework through which everything he or she does can have meaning and make sense.

The activation of these deep energies by events in our family of origin stimulates a profound readiness or expectancy for perfect experiences of (1) parenting, (2) emotional companionship and personal development, (3) power and freedom, and (4) meaning or purpose.

How Psychological Stages of Development Contribute to Healthy Adulthood

Psychologist Erik Erikson's psychosocial theory asserts that four specific stages of development occur during childhood, and four parallel stages take place during the rest of our lives.[2] Each of Erikson's stages is negotiated as a part of the process of becoming a whole human being. If we successfully negotiate these "crisis points," we develop toward wholeness. If not, we arrive at adulthood wounded or dysfunctional in some way. Fortunately, it is possible as adults to renegotiate these stages as a part of our recovery journey.

Each stage deals with two opposite forces—positive and negative, or functional and seemingly dysfunctional—which must be *integrated* within a person for optimum growth to occur. In Erikson's terms, the childhood stages are (in order): trust versus mistrust, autonomy versus shame or doubt, initiative versus guilt, and industry versus inferiority. Just as identical poles of two magnets being pushed together generate a field of tremendous tension and force, so a similar inner tension is felt by the child during the process of integrating the opposites, such as trust and mistrust, at each growth stage. When the opposites are sufficiently reconciled, there is a release of energy (much like the merging of two swiftly flowing rivers), which provides the impetus for moving to the next stage.

We evidently encounter the first side of each paradoxical stage of development with the activation of our deep longing. For example, trust comes from the activation of our longing for perfect, trustworthy care givers. As we work with our longing in a less-than-perfect environment, we confront the opposite side of the paradox. Mistrust comes when our less-than-perfect care givers disappoint us. Dealing with this dual experience of the inner longing and the outer disappointments evokes a process in us that psychologists have called learning. Each developmental stage calls forth a specific learning process. Examples will be explored as each stage is described.

Psychological growth is paradoxical, involving the combination of seeming opposites. Healthy growth also involves going forward to successive stages of development, not regressing to previous stages. As we go forward toward each new developmental stage, we enter into the mystery of having to surrender precisely what we've clung to the most during the previous stage. In Erikson's developmental theory, a person must surrender the principal strength developed during any stage so that entering into the emerging strength of the following stage is possible.

This paradox is illustrated in the dilemma of Abraham, who was torn between the Semitic tribal custom of offering the firstborn son as a sacrifice to God, and his love for his only son, whom God had promised would be the father of a large nation. If Abraham killed his son, he would lose the promise; if he did not kill his son in sacrifice, he would disobey the angel of God (a religious prompting of archetypal intensity). In faith, Abraham followed God into the paradox. At the very moment he was to sacrifice his son, Abraham realized (again with angelic or archetypal intensity) that the sacrifice was to be internal instead of external, a spiritual sacrifice of detachment instead of a physical killing. This internal sacrifice moved Abraham to a whole new level of spiritual development. A parallel example for today is the paradox of giving up control of one's teenager or "adult child" so that a healthy relationship is possible. This requires surrendering the kind of parenting a younger child may need so that the next phase of parent-child relating can emerge.

Accomplishing the Developmental Tasks Activates Contact Points and Their Energy Patterns

The experiences encountered in childhood developmental stages serve to activate the four contact points described in chapter 2, releasing their adaptive energy patterns. In addition to the energy, a child receives intuitive "information" from the contact point about what to expect, and a set of inborn responses that guide his or her behavior. The energy released from each activated contact point during the four developmental stages implants within the child, stage by stage, the deep longings for security, emotional companionship, power and freedom, and meaning or purpose. He or she then unconsciously measures the actual experience of his or her developmental stage against the yearning created by the ideal image of each contact point.

Now we begin to weave the strands of our basket together. The chart in Figure 1 shows the relationship between the natural characteristics of a child, the four contact points described, and the developmental stages of childhood. These first three strands interact with and amplify each other.

Natural Characteristic	Contact Point	Developmental Stage
Neediness and Dependence	Yearning for Perfect Parenting	Trust vs Mistrust
Vulnerability	Yearning for Perfect Companionship and Emotional Development	Autonomy vs Shame & Doubt
Imperfection	Yearning for Perfect Power and Freedom	Initiative vs Guilt
Immaturity	Yearning for Perfect Meaning and Perspective	Industry vs Inferiority

Figure 1: Parallels Between Growth Models

As we've seen, contact points, when activated, provide us with energy, information, and inborn responses to the information. When a child confronts a new developmental task along the growth path, the tension created by the new challenge activates the contact point within the child, bringing on a tremendous burst of energy with which to approach the new task, information about how to go about it, and a ready-made set of behaviors to apply to it. The four contact points and their energy patterns contribute to the healthy development of the child as he or she negotiates the developmental tasks described by Erikson.

I. TRUST VERSUS MISTRUST

The first of Erikson's developmental tasks is encountered between birth and eighteen months. The infant's task is to learn trust and to be open to being cared for by the parent. The shadow side of this process is mistrust. It needs to be integrated into the overall ability to trust. That is, the child learns that sometimes care givers aren't there exactly when needed. Putting the two traits together generates enough energy to move the child to the next developmental stage of dealing with autonomy, as the child learns a little more self-reliance.

The family-of-origin experience that allows the child to develop trust is a sense of bonding with the care giver, which activates the contact point and energy pattern of yearning for *perfect parenting*. A child, especially an infant, is needy and dependent. The principal task at this stage of life is to rely on the parents for basic survival. It's as if a child gets jump-started by this deep inner energy to be able to ask or signal for things and move toward his or her parents. Parents are the appropriate source of at least a certain amount of nurture. The profound power of the release of this deep longing for the parent enables the child to respond to the parenting, and thereby receive the nurture he or she needs for survival.

2. AUTONOMY VERSUS SHAME AND DOUBT

The second developmental task is encountered between the ages of eighteen months and four years. The child's job is to develop autonomy, a sense of individual identity. The shadow side of this process is shame and doubt, which needs to be integrated into the overall sense of autonomy. That is, the child's sense of separateness needs to be balanced by taking in the reactions of care givers that have placed limits on the child's free, independent behavior. Autonomy, or separateness, without a healthy sense of social limits can lead to alienation or dysfunctional behavior.

The child's attempts to achieve separateness may fail and result in painful consequences at times, producing a sense of shame and also introducing doubt about whether to continue testing his or her separateness. Learning to tolerate the shame of failure through secure relationships with care givers provides the child with enough energy to overcome doubt and to move on to stage three, the development of initiative.

The family-of-origin experience that permits the child to develop autonomy is the allowing of the child to practice separateness from the care givers while still relating to them. The child learns that he or she doesn't lose his or her relationship with the care givers in the act of being separate. Learning this helps the child develop boundaries that contain his or her sense of being a separate entity.

Children are born without boundaries to protect themselves and their rights as persons of equal value within the family. This vulnerability allows them to receive love and awareness of others, to more easily absorb response patterns and mimic care givers and to grow from such encounters. This vulnerable encounter with the family of origin triggers the energy pattern and yearning for *perfect companionship* and emotional integrity within relationships, which leads to emotional growth and happiness.

The activation of this deep energy drives the child toward developing independence while giving the child an internal image of the value of vulnerability in relationships. The child wants to be open and to receive from the care giver while at the same time establishing boundaries to protect the self. Depending upon how the care giver demonstrates boundaries and respects the child's tender, new boundaries, the child both develops a sense of boundaries and forms first impressions about what kind of boundaries are necessary in relationships.

3. INITIATIVE VERSUS GUILT

A child deals with the third developmental task roughly between the ages of four and six. The task is to develop initiative, the ability to make choices and carry them out. The shadow side of this task is guilt. The child sometimes does something while exploring the environment that transgresses his or her value system, or the value system being modeled by the respected and beloved care giver, and he or she feels guilt. The child then integrates the trial-and-error exploration and the value system by learning to let guilt limit his or her initiative. The successful balancing of initiative and guilt gives the child the impetus to move into the fourth developmental stage dealing with industry, learning how to do things proficiently, without transgressing values.

The family-of-origin experience that permits the child to develop initiative occurs when he or she asserts himself or herself, explores the environment, and learns through trial and error. This process releases the energy pattern and yearning for *power and freedom*—and the beginning awareness of how to make things happen in the world. Through identification with care givers and peers, the child gradually becomes comfortable with being imperfect, realizing that making mistakes is simply part of the process of trial-and-error learning. He or she also learns how to be accountable for mistakes—by acknowledging them and making amends.

4. INDUSTRY VERSUS INFERIORITY

The fourth prepuberty developmental task surfaces at about age six and continues to puberty. The child's task is to develop what Erikson terms industry, learning to master the tools of each new setting that comes into his or her life.

The shadow side of this developmental task is what Erikson terms *inferiority*, meaning a sense of being overwhelmed and not knowing how to get along in one's environment. At certain points the child makes transitions from one whole reality field to a new one, from one setting to another. The child moves out of the family into the wider neighborhood and into the school. On completing each stage of education the child moves into a new grade, gets a new teacher, changes schools, and perhaps even moves to a different town. Each event leads to an experience of loss of context, a loss of meaningful connection.

If these transitions are properly negotiated, a sense of industry and mastery develops. The child learns to learn—to adapt and transfer knowledge from the old context into the new one.

If the child does not master the cues and tools of the new setting, he or she develops a sense of inadequacy and confusion, or inferiority, and may be too discouraged to learn how to get along in the new environment. This shadow side needs to be integrated into the overall ability for mastery, called *industry*. When the child is placed in a new context, he or she learns to tolerate the accompanying sense of inferiority, of not knowing how things are done, while the learning process takes place. The child integrates the sense of inferiority (inadequacy and confusion) into his or her repertoire of experiences and does not allow it to stop the process of industry—of learning how to learn.

The dilemma presented by a new and unfamiliar environment triggers the energy pattern and yearning for *perfect meaning or purpose* in one's life. The changes feel chaotic and off-center to the child, but in response he or she feels a tremendous inner drive to learn how to find out what is going on, to be able to operate competently in the new context. The child has a great deal of knowledge about his or her former environments, some of which can be transferred and some of which doesn't work in the new one.

Some adults who observe a child's fumbling with this learning-to-learn process are apt to call the child "immature," as if immaturity were a deficiency or failure. Yet the learning-to-learn process is one of the ways we gain increasing levels of maturity beginning in childhood and continuing throughout our lives. To experience immaturity in this context is not a failure but a natural part of the process of learning to grow up. It becomes a shortcoming when a person has not fully reconciled industry with inferiority, and remains stuck in the immature shadow side—inferiority (or not knowing how to get along in one's environment).

NOTES

1. Pia Mellody, with Andrea Wells Miller and J. Keith Miller, *Facing Codependence* (San Francisco: Harper San Francisco, 1989), pp. 61–73.
2. Erik Erikson, *Childhood and Society,* 2d ed. (New York: W. W. Norton, 1963).

4

When Activation of Our Soul's Contact Points Goes Awry

The ideal procedure for growth to maturity we've examined in the previous chapter is, unfortunately, not always what actually happens to us. The families in which we grow up are made up of human beings who are naturally imperfect. We encounter care givers at home, school, and elsewhere who lack the ability to appropriately nurture, affirm, or support us in childhood. Psychological, emotional, spiritual, or physical injuries often result. We don't experience perfect care giving, emotional closeness, use of power, and meaning.

A spiritual component within each of us becomes damaged in the process of growing up in a dysfunctional family. This spiritual component involves what happens on the inside of a person when the release of the energy pattern impels us toward encounters with our flawed care givers. The energy does not flow properly, but gets misdirected, distorted, or denied. Once these contact points are activated during our childhood, the resulting yearnings, fueled by the energy patterns, continue to affect us throughout our lifetime, drawing us toward objects or behaviors that are harmful and dysfunctional instead of fulfilling. For optimum recovery, the spiritual component needs recognition and healing just as much as the emotional and psychological factors.

When these intense energies are *misdirected,* we may focus all of our tremendous drive on something other than the intended object. For example, a child who doesn't get the support he or she needs to get along at a new school (yearning for power and freedom) may turn that energy into rebellious, chaotic behavior.

When the energies are *distorted,* we misinterpret the message about what will satisfy the yearning. We may turn away from the very thing that is meant to satisfy the yearning, believing that it will bring harm rather than satisfaction. For example, a child who is taught that people will let you down and can't be trusted (yearning for perfect parenting) may resolve never to risk friendship or falling in love. The same can be said about being taught that God is harsh and punitive, or that God demands perfection. If we were taught these things, we may turn away from God, or risk only guarded involvement, believing God to be a destructive entity rather than a saving one.

When the archetypal energy patterns are *denied,* we may try to stifle them or detach from them, believing that there is no point in yearning for fulfillment, since satisfaction for the yearning isn't available. For example, a child who does not get enough opportunities to become a distinct being (yearning for emotional companionship and personal development) may stop trying to become a separate individual in relationships with others, and meekly accept the dependent role given to him or her.

Dysfunctional Families Do Not Satisfy a Child's Deep Longings

Terry Kellogg, a drug and alcohol abuse counselor, appeared with John Bradshaw on Bradshaw's PBS television series, "Bradshaw on the Family." He and Bradshaw suggested that four kinds of harmful parenting produce dysfunctional adults: neglect, enmeshment, abuse, and abandonment.[1] (In this context, we use the term *abuse* to mean the ab-use of power, the wrong use of it.) Mellody, Bradshaw, and Kellogg all say that the child's failure to mature due to the experiences of neglect, enmeshment, abuse, and abandonment leads to codependence in adulthood.

It is important to note that this discussion is not meant to be "parent bashing." Parents are regular human beings who are imperfect. Yet parental imperfection has an impact on the powerful internal energies released in children at various times during their growth and development.

Now we are ready to weave a few more strands of the basket together. When a child's deep inner longings are activated and he or she receives inadequate or imperfect parenting, the child usually experiences the forms of injury set forth by Bradshaw and Kellogg. As we place these strands together, we see that the gap between the yearnings of the triggered energy pattern and the actual encounters within the family of origin often results in the experiences of neglect, enmeshment, abuse, and abandonment. Figure 2 illustrates this concept.

The *dependent and needy* child encounters a parent whose ability to nurture the child is inadequate; nevertheless, the child's inborn energy pattern that expects perfect parenting is triggered. This results in a difference between the inner image of what the child expects from a parent and the reality of that parent's actual attention to the child—what Bradshaw and Kellogg call the experience of *neglect*. Neglect stems from the fact that the care-giving system we have doesn't take care of us as we intuitively expect, but does things *other than* meet our needs. Neglect is distinct from abandonment, which is the absence of any care-giving system at all.

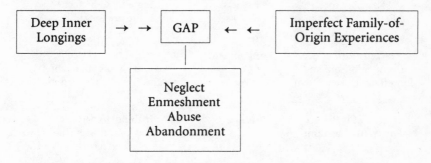

Figure 2: The Gap Between Deep Inner Longings and Imperfect Experiences
in the Family of Origin

The *vulnerable* child encounters a care giver whose ability to support the development of a separate identity is inadequate, yet the encounter triggers the child's instinctive longing for perfect companionship. The child experiences *enmeshment* when his or her care giver does not recognize and take into consideration the child's natural lack of boundaries, does not model and teach the child healthy boundaries, or both.

When the *imperfect* child's experiences trigger his or her longing for power and personal freedom, he or she may encounter one or more care givers with little or no tolerance for the child's need to explore reality through a trial-and-error process. Such a care giver does not assist the child to deal appropriately with the child's own imperfection. The care giver may even attack the child for his or her imperfection. The child often experiences this attack as punishment for exploring his or her environment—what Bradshaw and Kellogg call *abuse*. This misuse of power by the adult harms the child and teaches him or her to hide or distort imperfections. In the relationship with the adult, the child learns a distorted use of power (*ab-use* of power) rather than the proper use of it.

The *immature* child encounters care givers who cannot understand or appreciate the child at his or her age level, and who do not give affirmation, appropriate loving confrontation, or support for the child's current stage of development. Nevertheless, the child's deep inner drive is triggered to find the meaning and purpose for his or her life. The resulting encounter with nonsupportive parents leaves the child feeling disconnected, inadequate, and confused—the experience of *abandonment*.

Deep Inner Longings → →	GAP	← ← Imperfect Family-of-Origin Experiences
Yearning for Perfect Parenting	Neglect	Inability to perfectly nurture the child.
Yearning for Perfect Companionship and Emotional Development	Enmeshment	Inability to perfectly perceive child's vulnerability. Transgression of child's boundaries.
Yearning for Perfect Power and Freedom	Abuse	Inability to perfectly assist child to deal with child's own imperfection.
Yearning for Perfect Meaning or Purpose	Abandonment	Inability to perfectly understand and appreciate child at child's age level.

Figure 3: The Gap Between Deep Inner Longings and Form of Injury in the Family of Origin

How the Inner Drive Toward Family of Origin Contributes to the Injury

As a child enters each developmental stage, he or she must grapple with three simultaneously occurring circumstances:

1. the developmental task itself;
2. the energy, information, and set of inborn response coming from the activated contact point; and
3. the external family-of-origin experience.

First, a child enters a developmental stage and the corresponding contact point is triggered, providing energy, information, and a set of inborn responses to these experiences. Now this child feels the release of the profound energy that occurs at the right time in his or her life. But if the response of the parent is deficient, *the child may very well link the power of this energy pattern to the dissatisfying experience.* This linkage poses a dilemma. At times the child's inborn responses may be met insufficiently, resulting in the child experiencing too much pain or trauma. The child modifies the energy and inborn responses to alleviate the excessive pain and to survive the experience emotionally, mentally, and spiritually, as well as physically. While the child may survive, the energy has been *misdirected, distorted, or denied.*

Further, the adjustments the child makes due to the painful encounters in the family of origin may prevent him or her from being able to release the principal strengths in one or more stages. Erikson's theory indicates that when a person clings to things he or she has most relied on and doesn't or can't surrender them when a new stage unfolds, the individual feels bewildering pain. If this pain is not addressed, if fulfillment for the deep yearnings implanted in us is not found, we experience the pain of codependence in adulthood. And we often become compulsive and addictive in order to quiet that pain.

Doing therapy about family-of-origin experiences is necessary and good, and getting clean and sober from any addictions is also vital. But these approaches to healing the pain are usually not enough. It seems we need to address another root feeding the pain to enter optimum recovery. The distorted, denied, or misdirected natural responses arising from the release of deep energy patterns need to be redirected to their proper satisfier.

Childhood Developmental Stages

Now we are ready to weave together three more strands of our basket: (1) Erikson's childhood developmental stages, (2) the contact points triggered during the stages, and (3) the core symptoms of codependence as described by Pia Mellody. By doing this we can more easily trace the spiritual root of codependence as follows:

- we account for the impact of the family of origin on the activation of each contact point,
- we see how the energy from the activation of the contact points and the impact of the family of origin *combine* to mold a child's development toward codependence or wholeness.

Erikson pointed out the difficulties an adult might have if that person was unable to negotiate the stages of development. By looking at these adult difficulties and Pia Mellody's dysfunctional survival traits (which lead to adult core symptoms of codependence) it is possible to make some educated guesses about the dysfunctional experiences that happened in childhood. Erikson's and Mellody's descriptions of adult difficulties both point to the fact that codependence is a state of immaturity, or failure to develop at one or more developmental levels during childhood, leading to problems with identity, self-care, and intimacy.[2] (See Figure 4.)

Childhood Developmental Stage [3]	Contact Point Activated [4]	Family-of-Origin Experience [5]	Dysfunctional Survival Trait [6]
1. Trust vs Mistrust	Yearning for Perfect Parenting	Neglect	Too Dependent or Antidependent or Needless/Wantless
2. Autonomy vs Shame and Doubt	Yearning for Perfect Companionship and Personal Development	Enmeshment	Too Vulnerable or Invulnerable
3. Initiative vs Guilt	Yearning for Perfect Power and Success	Abuse	Good/Perfect or Bad/Rebellious
4. Industry vs Inferiority	Yearning for Perfect Meaning and Perspective	Abandonment	Overmature (Controlling) or Extremely Immature (Chaotic)

Figure 4: Relationship of the Activation of Contact Points and
Their Energy Patterns to Symptoms of Codependence

I. TRUST VERSUS MISTRUST

Even if a child's care givers are only minimally adequate and not fully functional, they can activate powerful responses within their child so that the child clings to his or her parents even when doing so is painful. When the *dependent and needy* child, propelled toward the parent by the longing for perfect parenting, finds too little connection, *both* the reaching out and the insufficient response create the experience of *neglect.*

According to Erikson, the failure of the parent to nurture the child sufficiently hinders the child's development of social attachment and may block the full development of sensory and motor functions—a "gut" kind of intelligence.[7] Pia Mellody indicates that when a child's parents are inadequate in nurturing a child's natural neediness and dependence, the child becomes either too dependent or else overly independent, or needless and wantless, which in turn becomes a core symptom of codependence—inability to take appropriate responsibility for one's own needs and wants.

2. AUTONOMY VERSUS SHAME AND DOUBT

The *vulnerable* child experiences *enmeshment* when the child, who is asserting independence and self-management in matters such as walking, toilet training, and eating, is overrun by a care giver's need system. The care giver makes the child conform to what the care giver needs, rather than being responsive to seeing what the child needs. When confronted with such parenting, the child gets the message that the only way to continue to relate is to allow oneself to be invaded, to conform to what the care giver demands.

The child's vulnerability is actually a mode of learning, allowing the child to independently absorb another person's style and to learn complex behavior through imitation. The natural learning style of this developmental stage is violated through enmeshment.

When a child's attempts to establish autonomy fail, he or she feels shame and begins to be uncertain about continuing to establish autonomy. It may become too painful for the child to be anything but an extension of the care giver's reality system, that is, who the child is told to be. The child experiences varying degrees of shame or doubt whenever the need for expressing his or her individuality encounters boundary invasion by someone else.

If the care giver disregards the need for the child to develop a boundary system, the child never gets a sense of his or her own boundaries. The parent's failure to permit the child to develop boundaries and autonomy leads to the child's impairment in areas of physical movement, fantasy and play, language development, and self-control.[8] Pia Mellody suggests that when parents do not properly protect the child's vulnerability, the child becomes either too vulnerable or invulnerable. This in turn becomes a core symptom of codependence—the inability to set appropriate boundaries.

Again, the pain of this situation is fueled from the *outside in* by the parent's overrunning the vulnerable child's need to establish autonomy. It is also fueled from the *inside out* by the child's deep longing for affirming companionship and the yearning to be touched but not enmeshed so that the child can know that he or she exists.

3. INITIATIVE VERSUS GUILT

The *abuse* the *imperfect* child experiences when a care giver cannot deal with the child's inner need for power, personal initiative, and freedom harms the child and teaches him or her that it is not acceptable to explore the environment, and that he or she needs to hide or distort imperfections in order to avoid the abuse.

When the child's imperfection is met with inappropriately harsh or too frequent punishment, the child is led to fear the very urge to try things out. The lesson for the child could be, "The only way I know I have initiative is when I get punished." If the domination and punishment continue, the message could become, "The only way I know I exist is when I get punished." And then, "The only way I know that my needs are being met is when I get punished." These skewed messages build on one another.

According to Erikson, the experience of *abuse* (overcontrol, domination, punishment, and so forth) from care givers causes one of two opposite reactions. On the one hand, the child's initiative and sense of freedom is crushed, and he or she will learn not to try. In this case, the child just accepts someone else's definition of how he or she ought to explore the environment, and the child's "self-starting" is quashed. On the other hand, the child may reject teaching, regulations, limits, or guidelines, and defy authority at nearly every opportunity, in a desperate attempt to protect his or her freedom. Either way, such children are affected in the areas of sex-role identification, early moral development, ability to enjoy group play, and self-esteem.[9] Pia Mellody suggests that a care giver's attacks of a child's right to be imperfect, to commit errors in a trial-and-error process, gives the child the message that it is abnormal to be imperfect. The child responds in one of two ways. Either the child tries to become perfect and avoid errors (overcontrol of behavior) or the child concludes it's impossible to live up to the care giver's demand for perfection and becomes rebellious (undercontrol of behavior). This leads to the adult codependent symptom of difficulty owning and expressing one's own thoughts, feelings, or behavior, and difficulty acknowledging imperfection.

4. INDUSTRY VERSUS INFERIORITY

Abandonment is the experience of the *immature* child whose nonaffirming, nonsupportive parents leave him or her feeling disconnected, inferior, and confused.

According to Erikson, if the child did not successfully complete integrating the fourth developmental stage, industry versus inferiority, he or she has difficulty mastering the tools of new situations, doesn't know how to find out what is going on, and has little or no ability to make friends, to evaluate the self accurately, learn skills, and play on teams.[10] Pia Mellody suggests that when the immature child is not properly parented, he or she becomes either overmature (controlling) or remains extremely immature (chaotic and off center).

Carried Feelings and Inner Energy Patterns

Pia Mellody has written clearly and helpfully about the phenomenon called "carried feelings." She says that when a child is in the presence of a care giver who is in denial of, or acting irresponsibly with, his or her feelings, these feelings are induced in the child and carried forward into adulthood by that child. The child experiences these feelings as overwhelming, irrational, and reflexlike. When the child becomes an adult, the old feelings fire off in conjunction with current feelings the adult is having about something occurring in the present. It's hard for the person to figure out where these feelings are coming from, why they are so intense, or how to "control" them.

The theory of energy patterns can help explain the phenomenon of "carried feelings." Generally, a person experiences intense emotion when a contact point with its energy patterns is activated. This seems to support what Mellody says about the intense feelings a child has when he or she is in the vicinity of care givers who are out of control or being irresponsible with their emotions.

One of the reasons the child's experience may be so intense is that the care giver is just enough of a stimulus that an energy-pattern is activated inside the child, endowing the particular encounter with tremendous power. Anthony Stevens, in his book *Archetypes,* calls this experience the "innate releasing mechanism" (IRM). For example, when the child faces his or her father, the image the child has of the father has great power since it reflects the activation of the inner contact point and the accompanying energy-filled expectation of perfect parenting. Thus, the child's father seems (to the child) to carry all fatherhood, all that the child would want in terms of masculine authority, approval, protection, care giving, and so forth. When the actual father is in denial about his feelings, or acting irresponsibly with them, two things happen. First, the child is being conditioned from the outside (as Mellody describes). Second, the child experiences the activation of a tremendous expectancy and a readiness to be open to something greater than the child from the inside. The child may experience the release of these internal energies just at the time the father is dealing with his own feelings inappropriately. The father's dysfunctional expression of emotion somehow gets connected to the child's energy pattern. But the child still yearns for connection to loving masculine authority, and moves toward the father, even if the father is behaving dysfunctionally.

One of the Ten Commandments can provide some help here. The commandment "Honor your father and your mother" is not simply a guideline for acknowledging and obeying parents (who may sometimes act dysfunctionally). At a deeper level, the commandment calls us to honor our *deep yearning* for perfecting parenting, our search for connection to the Source of all life, authority, and nurture.[11]

Discovering How to Reconnect to God's Contact Points Within Us

We have an amazing capacity to recover from damage that occurs when our growth experience doesn't follow an ideal plan. Just as our physical selves heal when wounded, so can our emotional selves, our psychological selves, and our spiritual selves heal from injuries.

This healing capacity, even for our bodies, has not yet been duplicated in the laboratory. Even the most sophisticated doctors can supply only supportive help to the physical body. They can create the best atmosphere for it to heal itself, then stand by and watch to see if the mysterious healing process will happen.

By examining our own experiences along our growth path in childhood, we can identify our own damaged spiritual contact points and then begin to enter into a process to redirect, untwist, or reconnect to our misdirected, distorted, or denied archetypal energies.

Our Creator made allowances for the fact that we are born into an imperfect world, by providing the potential for healing in all aspects of ourselves: physical, emotional, psychological, and spiritual. This healing involves being in contact somehow with this Creator God.

NOTES

1. John Bradshaw, *Bradshaw on the Family* (Deerfield Beach, FL: Health Communications, Inc., 1988).
2. John Friel and Linda Friel, *Adult Children: The Secrets of Dysfunctional Families* (Deerfield Beach, FL: Health Communications, Inc., 1988) contains additional comments on Erikson and codependence.
3. Erik Erikson, *Childhood and Society,* 2d ed. (New York: W. W. Norton, 1963).
4. Anthony Stevens, *Archetypes* (New York: Quill Press, 1983).
5. John Bradshaw, "Bradshaw on the Family," PBS Telecast, 1987.
6. Pia Mellody, with Andrea Wells Miller and J. Keith Miller, *Facing Codependence* (San Francisco: Harper San Francisco, 1986).

7. Barbara M. Newman and Philip R. Newman, *Development Through Life: A Psychosocial Approach,* 4th ed. (Chicago: Dorsey Press, 1987), p. 33.
8. Newman and Newman, p. 33.
9. Newman and Newman, p. 33.
10. Newman and Newman, p. 33.
11. Edward F. Edinger, *The Bible and the Psyche* (Toronto: Innca City Books, 1986), pp. 62–63.

5

Recovering the Healthy Power of Activated Contact Points

The activation of our soul's contact points often goes awry. At an experiential level this may be a way to describe that fundamental religious problem called original sin in previous ages. We experience profound longings and expectations for fulfillment, and yet find a process within ourselves by which our actual life experiences fall short of bringing fulfillment. We feel alienated from other people, incomplete within ourselves, and cut off from God.

Spiritual Healing Is Vital

If a part of the origin of codependence is spiritual, then recovery needs to include spiritual elements. As adults, we may attempt to do our very best with self-help books, therapy, lectures, seminars, and even general support groups. And some relief does come from these processes, which help us alleviate feelings we may have absorbed from care givers in the past and build healthy boundaries to protect ourselves from absorbing feelings from others in the present.

But although we are really doing our best, we may still experience the overwhelming feelings within ourselves. Even worse, the urgent unmet longings and deep promptings seem to set us up for dysfunctional, self-defeating experiences again and again. It's as if the yearnings of our own deepest nature set us up. These persistent deep feelings may well be due to unrequited energy patterns— longings that were activated but not satisfied over the course of our lives.

The question is: *are the longings simply lingering immaturity or is there some way that they can be satisfied?* We believe these spiritual longings *can* be satisfied.

Getting into *proper* contact with the deep, powerful energies that rise up *within us* is absolutely necessary, we believe, for *full* recovery.

Acknowledging Our Longings and Our Painful Lack of Satisfaction

When we begin to face the frustration of our deep longings, the goal is not to get rid of the inner ideal, but rather to come out of denial about *the existence of the gap* between this ideal and the reality of our parents' inadequacy and flaws.

Many people get the idea that they must get rid of their ideal expectations because such ideals are "sick," and only serve to set us up for disappointment. Freud's answer was that God doesn't really exist and that believing in God is the pursuit of an illusion. *By contrast, Jung kept saying that the yearnings are important and necessary and that there is something beyond ourselves that can ultimately satisfy them.*

When we come out of denial, we can say, "This *is* the ideal I hungered for, but my experience was other than ideal, and there was a gap. Because of this gap, I am the way I am today. Now I'm going to learn how to mature, how to develop other resources for meeting this deep longing besides my past inadequate experience."

To become aware that we are functioning in the gap area, we must review our childhood experiences. We touch the feelings and memories from these experiences, and we touch our fear of these hungers. Reexperiencing all the unmet longings is painful to varying degrees, and it is often frightening. We do have a choice. We can either disqualify the longing (say it isn't there) in order to escape the pain of going back and touching the experience of living in the gap, or we can move forward into the pain toward deeper healing.

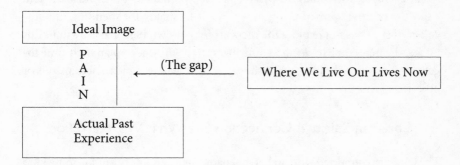

Figure 5: The Painful Experience of Living in the Gap

An Example of Proper Contact with an Inner Energy Pattern

Perhaps one of the most easily recognizable energy patterns released by the activation of a contact point is that of falling in love with someone. Artists often channel this powerful energy into something creative, such as painting or poetry.

When Dante first saw Beatrice,[1] he was awestruck; his knees turned to jelly. He was astonished not just by her physical beauty but by everything that the way she looked and the way she acted suggested. It was as though she contained within herself everything from the past that he could have possibly experienced about Woman and everything that was possible in the future.

His meeting with Beatrice triggered an energy pattern within Dante himself—what the Jungians call the *anima*, the image of the feminine. Dante then went home . . . and wrote a poem! He knew what he had experienced was not just that particular young woman; something had been triggered that was much larger than that external encounter. His relationship to that image was one of awe and even reverence, and it elicited in him a poetic outpouring. And so he properly directed those energies into poetic and artistic production.

Those of us without poetic or artistic talents can also channel such energies properly—into an appropriate expression of a part of ourselves. Such channeling doesn't mean that we don't enter a real relationship with the person we encounter. We may enter an external relationship if it is appropriate, but we also need to relate to the power of the energy pattern in a way that has meaning for our own personal growth. A danger is that we will ignore the *inner* message we are receiving via this relationship, and the intense energy will overpower and perhaps even destroy the external relationship with the person. In such an instance the relationship might not be a healthy one but perhaps a love-addicted relationship based on fantasy rather than reality.

For example, a wife may be attracted to the spontaneity of her husband and enjoy the creative spur-of-the-moment plans he makes for spending time together. If she does not explore the message for her own personal growth in this image, she may come to *demand* him always to be the one to plan their time together—until he is drained, while she never risks making a plan, spontaneous or otherwise, herself.

Christian Spiritual Connection Fits What We Yearn For

The longings connected with archetypal patterning energy cry out for some kind of answer. Many people have found an answer in Christianity. Practical contact with this patterning energy, the "messengers from God," does occur in our daily lives, but it can also be experienced through religious rituals, prayer, and spiritual direction, which are the spiritual means offered by mainstream Christian traditions throughout the centuries. The Twelve Steps of Alcoholics Anonymous have also proved to be an effective pathway toward this end, guiding people to a constant turning over of their lives to the Source and proper Satisfier of these great internal forces.

In one of the earliest autobiographies ever written, the *Confessions*,[2] St. Augustine describes himself as a very compulsive person and a love addict. He came to a conclusion after a lifetime of being compulsive: "Our hearts are made for you, O God and they cannot rest until they rest in You." This, we believe, is a central secret to understanding the nature of compulsion.

Even as we engage in our compulsions, we say, "This isn't going to satisfy what I long for, but it's the best I've got." Historically, this mind-set has been called *idolatry*. That is why the First Commandment is necessary for recovery and wholeness (Exod. 20:1).

> You shall not have other gods besides me. You shall not have idols for yourselves in the shape of anything in the sky above or the earth below or the waters beneath the earth. You shall not bow down before them or worship them. For I the Lord your God am a jealous God . . .

"Worship" as used in this verse can be translated as the conscious directing of our deepest energies to God alone. When we disregard this reality we may experience unrequited longings in ourselves and across several generations. But the commandment also promises restoration in recovery, ". . . to the thousandth generation" to those who love God and keep the commandments.

The spiritual tradition of Christianity has long advocated that we must ultimately aim our deepest yearnings somewhere that *cannot fail* in terms of care giving, love and companionship, power, and meaning. If we do not so aim, our own ego controls enter, and we try to force external relationships and objects to fulfill our deepest inner longings. Our attempts to recreate the world according to our expectations lead us to become compulsive. The Christian spiritual tradition says that the only fail-proof satisfier for our deepest yearnings is God.

From one point of view, the Christian doctrine of the Trinity, three Persons in one God, addresses the four deep longings we have described. First, our making *proper* contact with God, the Father (Parent), addresses the pain of our experience of neglect by our major care givers. We are encouraged to believe that God truly cares for our welfare and can meet our longing for perfect *parenting*. Second, when we meet God, the Son (Child), Emmanuel, who is with us, loving us and healing us in real human relationship, we have met the proper object for *love and companionship* that heals the pain of enmeshment. Third, when we have met the Holy Spirit who is known through works, gifts, and manifestations of God's actions, we can satisfy our deepest yearning for *power and freedom* in this world, and healing from the pain of experienced abuse. Fourth and finally, when we enter into the mystery of the Trinity dwelling within us, we have at our center a *meaning* that does not change, and we can heal from the pain of our experiences of meaninglessness and abandonment.

Learning to Tolerate Paradox Is Crucial to Recovery

As we mentioned earlier, Erik Erikson's developmental theory is paradoxical: we must surrender precisely what we relied on the most at one level to move on to the next level. As we move to each new level, it's as if nearly everything that we've known goes away and we are on uncharted ground once again. This experience sometimes feels almost like being annihilated. To grow through the various developmental tasks, we must find a way to tolerate this particular experience of abandonment, of life as we know it going away. We must have something deeper to sustain us that never changes. Being in contact with that something helps us keep moving forward in growth. The indwelling Trinity is there no matter what, although it is often hard for us to believe it because of our difficulty disentangling our experience with imperfect human beings from the reality that a truly dependable Higher Power is there for us.

Coping with Internal Contradiction

We have a deep sense that these urgent archetypal longings in us are true and real, and even more importantly, we believe that somehow they can be satisfied. But at the same time we encounter the apparently contradictory, imperfect conditions of real life that demand our attention. How do we deal with them both?

As we turn these deepest longings toward God, we begin our spiritual recovery—also called our conversion, or the working out of salvation. Somewhere in this process we eventually realize that the thing we knew could answer the deepest yearnings of our heart really exists! At that point, we experience a great joy that cannot be taken from us. These yearnings *can* be filled after all. This fulfilling of our longing in a uniquely personal way is our coming to completion. We can now see our real life experiences, our mistakes, and our physical imperfections as an expression of our longings, a part of our unique selves. We realize God loves us *as we are,* precisely because of the "wrinkles and bumps" that make us unique individuals. This increasingly conscious working out of our individuality, in

connection with a power greater than ourselves, is what Jung called "individu-
ation."

We Participate in Healing, but We Do Not Heal Ourselves

But there is a dilemma. If we admit that even doing our very best with self-help
is not enough, and then surrender our lives to God, what *active* part do we take
in confronting and using the strong creative powers surging up from the deepest parts of us? The solution to the dilemma seems to be a very fine line: we neither deny that these energies exist, nor do we claim the energies as merely an
extension of ourselves. In other words, we must stay in conscious relationship with
the inner energies and this power but know that *we* are not the basis of this
power. In fact, although the powerful energy pattern resides in the deepest part
of us, it is not just for us, but is a *contact point* with the power of God.

Sometimes people have wanted to revise the Seventh Step of Alcoholics Anonymous from "Humbly asked God to remove these shortcomings" to "Cooperated
with God in removing these shortcomings." This revision in the Seventh Step's
wording may be an attempt to acknowledge the necessity of having an active role
in confronting the misdirection, distortion, or denial of these energies within us.

Of course, our conscious will does not go away in recovery, nor are we totally
passive. The intent of the steps isn't for us to be inactive. We cooperate and allow;
this is an active process. But at the same time, it doesn't seem possible to be
healed at a spiritual level on our own, without connecting to the power of God.
Another way of saying this is that our *active* role involves straightening out the
direction of these profound longings within us, these contact points to God.

Our Active Role Is to Seek the Kingdom of God

The recovery movement has begun to emphasize getting in touch with our inner
child of the past—to find the place where our deep energy patterns were first
misdirected and to redirect the energies to the proper target. Contacting the
inner child of the past is reminiscent of Jesus' words in Matthew, "Unless you become like little children you shall not inherit the Kingdom of God" (Matt. 18:3),
and also his commandment in the New Testament to "seek first the Kingdom of
God and all its justice and these things shall be given unto you" (Matt. 6:33).

First Jesus says that unless we become as little children, we will not enter the
Kingdom of God. He also notes that these truths are revealed "to the merest
children" and remain hidden "to the learned and wise" (Matt. 11:25). Therefore, connecting to our inner child of the past and staying in touch with the joy

and pain of this connection will help us find a way to allow spiritual connection to God to occur.

An important meaning of *justice* in the context of these quotations is "correct relationship," the ordered, appropriate fulfillment of one's covenant or one's proper relationship. So one way to "seek the Kingdom of God" may be to go about properly ordering to God the deep energy patterns from our activated contact points. *The New World Dictionary Concordance to the New American Bible Commentary* says that the word *justice* had the nuance of the Savior-king bringing an intervention from the outside for the benefit of the citizens. A warrior-king in the time of Christ would conquer a land and establish justice. Such justice was aimed at the happiness and prosperity of the inhabitants of the realm of the king. God's justice is God establishing a Spiritual reign, further revealing a reality that has been within us all along. It is a saving action by God that is salvation for the Christian. For a person in a Twelve-Step community, the Third Step calls one into God's reign—turning our life and our will over to the care of God as we understand God. According to the book *The Twelve Steps and Twelve Traditions,* this surrender is the only proper use of *our* will; the rest has got to be *God's* will.[3]

Several parables about the Kingdom of God or Kingdom of Heaven in the New Testament have information for us. We can gain new insight by reading the Gospel of Matthew, substituting the word *recovery* for *Kingdom of God* or *Kingdom of Heaven* wherever we find it. For example, Matthew 5:3, "Blessed are the poor in spirit, for theirs is the Kingdom of Heaven" might be read as "Blessed are the poor in spirit, for theirs is *recovery.*" This interpretation can speak powerfully to our modern, addicted, and codependent culture.

The Gospels give us powerful similes to help us grasp what is meant by "the Kingdom of God," translated as "recovery." Jesus says in Matthew that the Kingdom of God (recovery) is like a treasure buried in a field. A man finds the treasure and goes to sell everything he has to buy that field (Matt. 13:44). Or, the Kingdom of Heaven (recovery) is like a merchant searching for fine pearls. When he finds one pearl of great price, he sells all he owns to buy that pearl (Matt. 13:45–46). In the Orient, the spherical, perfect quality of the pearl was often seen as the symbol of the soul. Connecting to the deepest longings of our soul makes us aware of the pearl of great price, the most valuable thing we could ever imagine—our connection to God. Seeking the Kingdom of God, then, involves developing a life around responding to God's offer of connection to us that keeps us in our right mind—a life in recovery.

Jesus addresses our deep need for security when he says, "Why are you afraid you're not going to get food and clothes? Seek first the Kingdom of God (recovery) and its *justice*." When we can do this, all other things will be given to us in addition.

Beginning the Quest for Proper Connection to God

Each one of us had unique relational experiences in childhood that formed the adults we are today. Universal, powerful, inner yearnings were also operating within us. To find deeper levels of recovery we need to find the place or places to which our inner energy patterns were first misdirected, so that we can redirect the energies to the proper target. The next section helps us begin to pinpoint some of these places.

NOTES

1. Dante Alighieri, *The New Life* (La Vita Nuova) in *The Portable Dante,* Paolo Milano, ed. New York: Viking Press, 1947.
2. *The Confessions of St. Augustine,* translated by E. M. Blaiklock. New York: Thomas Nelson Publishers, 1983.
3. *The Twelve Steps and Twelve Traditions* (New York: Alcoholics Anonymous World Services, Inc., 1952), p. 40.

Part II

Assessment

6

Discovering Where We Need
Spiritual Healing

Often those of us who have experienced neglect, enmeshment, abuse, or abandonment in childhood are not fully aware of this because of psychological defense
mechanisms such as denial, delusion, suppression, repression, or dissociation,
which block important aspects of our past from our present awareness. We use
these defense mechanisms to lock away painful memories and to protect ourselves
at a fundamental level. We first used them at a time in our lives in which we
were small and helpless, didn't have options or resources, didn't think really
well, and feared we could be annihilated.

During experiences of neglect, enmeshment, abuse, or abandonment, we as
children are overwhelmed by our own feelings, especially when they are combined with those introjected from the care giver. These feelings overwhelm us
from within as well as from without. For protection, we split off the overwhelming feelings, either by repression or dissociation. The early memory,
complete with the forceful emotions, goes into storage in our unconscious
mind, perhaps as a body memory, a pictorial memory, a verbal memory, or a
feeling memory. These potentially explosive "time capsules" remain in our unconscious mind, ticking away.

We grow up. Whenever a current situation occurs that is similar enough to
something painful we experienced in childhood, the emotional aspect of the
memory stored in our unconscious mind can erupt, *whisking us back to past
emotions* as if we were travelers in a time machine. We experience the intensity
of childhood emotional reactions—diffuse, overwhelming, black-and-white.
We often feel shamed as well as overwhelmed, and we are reluctant to examine
or reveal what is behind our emotional outburst. We may also behave childishly,

acting out these old, powerful feelings, and then we may experience even less willingness to look at or share this secret about our past.

How to Recognize the Eruption of Old Childhood Feelings

By evaluating what is going on in our adult lives, we can get a glimmer that perhaps we experienced abandonment, neglect, abuse, or enmeshment in childhood.

We often recognize these collisions with old childhood feelings because they seem to amplify everyday feelings in a mysterious way. In the midst of an especially intense outburst, we may wonder, "Why am I so mad about this little thing? Or so hurt, or so afraid?" It's quite possibly one of our painful childhood "time capsules" bursting open.

Old childhood issues may also come up at certain times when we're raising children. Raising our children allows us to review our feelings about our own childhood experiences. As we make the effort to relate to a child by connecting to his or her emotional frame of reference, we are at the same time connecting to our own family-of-origin experience at that age. We are likely to encounter a buried memory from our own childhood projected onto our own children. For example, perhaps one of our children, who previously seemed to be well balanced and delightful, begins to get on our nerves. Or perhaps we discover we can't relate to one of the children anymore, and we don't know why that child has changed so much.

Instead of trying to control the child, the question we should ask ourselves is, "What was going on with me in my family at this age?" For example, when parents find that their child is driving them crazy and they come in for counseling, it's almost common wisdom among therapists to ask the parents to communicate with each other about what was going on in their respective families of origin when they were the age of the child. When the parents begin to do this, the child sometimes stops misbehaving because—as strange as it seems—it is as if the child was unconsciously acting as a mirror to help Mom or Dad complete a growth task or solve an unconscious problem. But when the *parent* takes responsibility for the growth task or for solving the problem, the child's mission is over. He or she doesn't have to play the role of parental mirror anymore.

Why We Need to Review Our Past

We need to examine our childhood memories because it takes continuing energy to block off the painful emotions that are being evoked by day-to-day occurrences. Blocking emotions uses up our available energy needed to deal

RECOVERING CONNECTIONS

with our life properly. If we're having to keep these memories or emotions locked away, our options are limited. We may avoid certain situations, actions, or experiences that are similar to traumatic events in childhood and not know that we're in a pattern of avoidance. We may screen out certain perceptions because they might be too upsetting. We may refuse to feel certain feelings, becoming disconnected from our emotional life in adulthood. In all these situations we are cut off from many healthy forms of satisfaction and fulfillment. We're not living a full life with the capacity to grow spiritually.

For our children's sake, we need to heal from our own past psychological and emotional injuries. We can better avoid passing problems on to our children, or remove our children from the position of having to illustrate them for us by becoming compulsive and acting out, dramatizing for us what we will not look at in ourselves.

Facing the reality of how our legitimate, natural, deep longings were not fulfilled by our family of origin, and entering the pain such acknowledgments brings, begins the healing journey. In addition to refraining from addictions and addressing our childhood family-of-origin issues, we need to *seek satisfaction for our deepest longings in appropriate places.* This additional aspect of recovery provides deeper serenity and brings us back in touch with the power and energy available to us from the inner contact points implanted in us by our Creator.

Our spiritual need can best be met by a *spiritual remedy.* Our deep spiritual longings can be filled by directing our energies toward a relationship with God in these four ways:

1. God the Parent can provide us with the care and nurture for which we yearn. (See chapter 15.)
2. Jesus Christ (God's child) is the Perfect Companion who accompanies us on our life's journey and can teach us how to develop healthy boundaries, make healthy choices, and use our projection experiences as road maps into greater self-awareness. (See chapter 19.)
3. The Holy Spirit teaches us the proper use of power as we become aware of the action of God in our lives. (See chapter 23.)
4. The Trinitarian God—the Parent, the Child, and the Holy Spirit, who dwells within us—can teach us how to find meaning even though we may experience painful losses or confusing changes. (See chapter 27.)

Deterrents to Unlocking the Secrets of Our Pasts

We Americans aren't a particularly reflective people. We've been busy building up a vast country and conquering external frontiers, and we're not very introspective. We're very present- and future-oriented people, not past-oriented or traditional people. We don't seem to like looking at the past. One disadvantage of this is that we seem to need to relearn the same lessons over and over again. So we need help and prompts to be able to look inside ourselves.

In particular, there are at least three dynamics at work within us that seek to keep buried the vital information we need. One is that our memory is adaptive to our present situation, that is, it helps preserve our life here and now. Our difficulty remembering painful things is adaptive because these memories are tiring and distracting.

A second dynamic is the sense of shame that accompanies the memories, giving the message that we are somehow inadequate, or failures, whenever we have "childish" emotional outbursts. Because our sense of shame gives us a desire to hide, we have difficulty reviewing certain areas of our lives. Many of the memories are unconscious or preconscious. Except for overreacting to situations and reexperiencing these childhood feelings, we normally don't feel the pressure to go back into the memories themselves.

A third inhibiting dynamic is related to our survival instinct. Neglect, enmeshment, abuse, and abandonment often occur at early stages in our lives, when our defense mechanisms have to do with our very survival. At that age, we believe we have to bury our feelings, conform to our care givers' wishes, or whatever else is called for, to survive. So later, in adulthood, when some of these childhood feelings kick loose in us, we may feel once more our very survival is threatened. We certainly don't want to dig them up again, because it still seems as if our *very lives* are at stake.

How Denial Works to Keep Painful Data
Out of Our Awareness

As children, we may hide evidence from ourselves about the parent that contradicts our ideal expectancy, as if to say, "No, I must have a parent that matches my longings, so this inadequacy in my parent cannot exist." The energy released within the child toward the parent is resourceful and very necessary in the child's life, but his or her actual experience has been disappointing, and the child "makes up the difference" in order to have a parent image that matches ideal expectations.

This is a factor in the origin of the defense mechanisms of denial and delusion. The unconscious message is something like, "No, this neglect, abuse, enmeshment, or abandonment isn't happening, because I need the kind of perfect parents I expected to have."

One adjustment many of us make is to deny that a gap exists between the perfect image we yearn for and the reality of who the parent is. Our thinking may be something like the following examples:

> My parents didn't neglect me. They were just busy because. . . . And we supply a reason: there were so many children, or not enough money, or demanding jobs, or important duties, or a physical handicap.
>
> My mother didn't enmesh with me. We just had a special, close kind of relationship. She wouldn't have made it if it weren't for me there helping her. My sisters envy my close relationship with my mother.
>
> My father didn't abuse his power. He was right to control me; he loved me and was afraid I would get hurt. Or my mother must have loved me a lot to pay such close attention to me and correct every little thing I did. She couldn't understand how much it hurt me and she wouldn't have done it if she'd known.
>
> My parents didn't abandon me. They wanted me to be self-reliant, and I got by just fine. I got taught everything I need to know.

The reality being denied is this: *such encounters with care givers were the occasion for a form of injury to the child.* If we want to begin the healing process concerning these injuries, it seems we must judge not by the intention of the care givers but by the impact on the child. The fact that parents may have loved the child and not been aware of doing any damage doesn't matter. Parents may truly have had too many demands on their time and too few inner resources to be able to give to the child whom they loved. However, the biggest obstacle to recovery is the child's (and later adult's) denial that injury resulted from such conditions in family life no matter how well-meaning the parents are.

In confronting our denial, it is helpful to remember that now, as adults, we have many more resources at hand to protect ourselves. First of all, we have an additional sense of support and power that comes from our growing relationship to God. When we do recover some of the memories, it is usually safe enough for us to finally integrate some of the painful feelings associated with them. The unconscious has its own time to give us this information. That may be the real meaning of Paul's statement that God doesn't give us any more than we can bear (1 Cor. 10:13). God provides the protection we need so that we can remember what we are ready to deal with, and leave the rest until the proper time.

Second, we have more mature thinking ability, greater ability to care for ourselves, and a trusted person or two to talk with about these issues. And third, we know that by entering into the pain of the past and working it through we dismantle childhood "time capsules," eventually stop them from erupting in our adult lives, and gradually free ourselves to utilize more of our emotions in productive ways in our present lives.

Connection to the Twelve-Step Recovery Process

This process of confronting our denial may be related to a Fourth Step inventory. The Fourth Step asks that we make a fearless and searching moral inventory of ourselves. Some people's major problem was expressed by acting out and injuring others. Perhaps recovery from codependence also requires an inventory of areas where *we* are injured or broken, where *we* feel shamed, where *we* don't feel like we represented ourselves adequately in many events in our lives. The Fourth Step can be a way of looking at the spiritual roots of our life situations.

The next four chapters contain checklists and questions about both your adult traits and behaviors and your childhood memories. Fill them out the best you can. If a question doesn't provoke an answer in you at this time, just skip it and do the ones you can. You may not remember certain things, and there may be good psychological reasons to remain unaware of them. It may be that as time goes on you will become more aware of information that will help you answer these items.

A Few Special Areas to Pay Attention To

Pay attention to any physical feelings you might have in your body when you're working through your memories. If any strong feelings come up, such as a pain in your right hand, your throat, or your groin, make a note of them.

Pay attention to reactions you may be having toward other people at the present time. For example, you may get very angry at your spouse, or you may feel distant from your children. You may feel insecure when your spouse is away for a period of time, or you may feel invaded when one of your kids wants your attention. Just make a note of these, and be aware of them. Usually when we start exploring the recovery of our childhood memories, we start experiencing things that seem at first to be external. By making note of them, we can take them in and relate to them ourselves. Keep in mind that parts of our present behavior eventually reveal much of this repressed material in the way it's projected in our relationships with people.

A Helpful Visualization for Unlocking Childhood Memories

If you have a hard time remembering much, try this visualization exercise. Sit quietly somewhere, and go back in your mind to the house or houses where you lived from your earliest memory up to the end of elementary school or to junior high school. If you moved a lot, pick the earliest house you can remember, then repeat this exercise for each house after that. If it's very frightening for you to do this, do it in the presence of someone you trust.

In your imagination, enter the house. Remember how the house smelled, what it looked like, what was on the wall, where the beds were, where you went to the bathroom, what kind of glasses and dishes and silverware you had meals with. Then visit your backyard, neighborhood, school building, classrooms, teachers, and places where you and your friends played or hung out.

When you start remembering all of these cues, the other memories that are linked to them often come back, too.

A Process Useful Both for Previously Recovered Memories and New

If you've answered some of these questions in therapeutic work you've done, you need not necessarily look for new examples. By bringing these past memories out here, you can apply spiritual healing to them. This may be especially helpful for issues that you've dealt with that keep coming back. Perhaps they keep coming back because they're archetypally fueled and need to be addressed spiritually. Although you may have dealt in therapy with the forces coming *at you from the outside,* from your care givers, now you can deal with rechanneling your *internal* energies around the same issues. We will apply messages from the Bible and the spiritual side of life to these issues.

You may also have remembered some new examples of these situations, because time has passed and you have more tools and more safety and can deal with things at different levels. So there may be a mixture of past examples and new memories.

7

Experiences of Neglect

One of the basic signs of childhood neglect is *unconsciousness*. That is, when we have experienced severe neglect, we have never been awakened to life itself. We are unconscious to ourselves and our lives to the degree that we experienced neglect—a mild degree or a more extreme degree. In extreme cases, it's as if we are not on the planet. No one has called us into being, into recognizing the particular unique person we really are, or that we have an independent existence. It's as though that little sparkle isn't there in our eyes. A severely neglected person may go all the way through college and get a very high degree of education, yet remain very unconscious about himself or herself apart from external expectations.

The way we take care of ourselves as adults is based on the kind of care we received as children. So if people didn't pay much attention to us then, it's pretty hard to pay attention to ourselves as adults.

We may have various forms of inconsistency in our self-care. For example, we may eat fairly well and have adequate clothes, but not go to the dentist or the doctor when we need to. Or, we may take good care of our medical needs but not buy adequate or appropriate clothing and perhaps be stingy regarding other basic needs for ourselves.

The first goal of our childhood development was to integrate *trust and mistrust*. Trust comes from the activation of our deep longing for perfect, trustworthy care givers. As we begin to work with this longing in a less-than-perfect environment, our trusted care givers disappoint us. We encounter mistrust.

If we do not complete this integration, we become locked into one of the two stances. Developing only trust leads toward gullibility or overdependence on others. Developing only mistrust leads toward cynicism and difficulty forming healthy, appropriate attachments to others. Some people may switch back and forth between gullibility and cynicism, or between trusting unsafe people and hiding from trustworthy ones. This shifting back and forth is an example of the adult symptom of codependence that Pia Mellody calls "living in extremes."

As we grapple with integrating trust and mistrust, this dual experience of the inner longing and the outer disappointments calls forth a learning process similar to *classical conditioning*.[1] Classical conditioning involves learning about how the world is actually structured and how to fit into that structure. In the classical conditioning process, the person is actively receptive and experiences events as they happen, connecting together the fundamental structure of reality.

The central fact we learn during the first eighteen months is how to interact with an existing structure that's supposed to take care of us. For example, the baby eventually learns by observation that mother comes back after mother leaves. This and other events teach the baby to trust that the structure will take care of him or her.

When we experience neglect, we don't know for sure whether the surrounding environment will support us, or, in more extreme cases, whether such a structure exists. This seems to set up the resulting basic insecurity felt by those of us who experience neglect.

If we did not get *enough* nurture as a child, we may continue to long for an experience of being filled and cared for as an adult. In our hearts, we yearn for someone to take care of us, to call us into awareness of ourselves. Something within our very souls drives us to seek perfect nurture in our lives from "out there somewhere." We continue to "set ourselves up" in our friendships, love relationships, and even in our jobs to expect someone or some institution—perhaps a church or corporation—to take care of us.

The result is that we have unrealistic expectations about how the people in our lives "should" meet this need. When enough people and institutions have "let us down" by failing to meet our need, we may then try turning away from the need itself, trying not to need others too much. We realize correctly that others cannot satisfy that deep longing for perfect nurture, yet we still experience discomfort as we try to live with the unmet need as if *no* satisfaction were possible. We ourselves can't satisfy the need, and in a sense we know that no one else is supposed to take care of us as much as our heart yearns for. So the hunger goes on, and we try to ignore it or grimly endure it.

Some persons may attempt to achieve relief from this inner drive through various addictions. Carol Roberts, who works in a drug rehabilitation center, asked recovering patients what effect they desired when they took drugs. Instead of focusing on *what drug they took,* Roberts based her treatment on the psychological effect *desired*, no matter what drug was taken. She found that the responses of the patients fell into four categories that seem to match the same four deep archetypal yearnings of the heart we have been discussing. These four categories are: desire for sedation, euphoria, stimulation, and escaping to another reality.

Building on her observation, it appears that those who have experienced neglect may be the ones who take drugs for their sedative effect. Sedatives help people get relief from the tension of being in constant need, and help them feel warm, full, cared for, and relaxed. But the harmful consequences from these drugs eventually catch up with people. The drugs are not a good solution to the yearning.

Roberts suggests that a person might find the same relaxing effect as from taking a sedative drug by participating in some of these activities: fishing, meditation, deep breathing, soaking in a Jacuzzi, reading, music, massage, appropriate sex, or sunbathing.[2] While these activities give the desired effect more slowly than the drugs themselves, Roberts's recommendations attempt to *fill the inner hunger that drove the person toward the drug* in the first place.

Coming out of the state of unconsciousness by entering recovery, or waking up to life as an adult, is difficult because to come out of unconsciousness means to get in touch with the fact that we have not really addressed our own needs, and this can be very painful to face. So it's often easier for us to remain unconscious most of our lives, not feeling the pain of unmet needs. The lack of attention from our family may *feel* familiar, and thus self-neglect may actually feel *safer* than self-care. At least we know what self-neglect feels like.

Adult Characteristics

Following are typical characteristics of adult behavior of people who experienced neglect from care givers in childhood. Read through the list and write in your journal any that pertain to you, or any others that seem to you to be connected to your experiences of neglect:

UNCONSCIOUSNESS

Indecision
Worry, feelings of fear
Tendency toward being passive
Overdependence on others
Difficulty being aware of my own needs
Difficulty taking care of myself

Difficulty asking others to help me meet my needs

Tendency to be easily taken in by others, or gullible

Difficulty assessing reality of situations

Feelings of rootlessness or not belonging

Difficulty with imagination

Difficulty remembering facts

Difficulty receiving compliments from others

Difficulty enjoying myself at home, work, or play

Difficulty receiving care giving from others

Tendency to be controlling and preemptive at work or in personal relationships

Tendency to be socially and emotionally detached

Usually underemployed

Sense of being unprepared for life

Frequent sickness with vague or shifting symptoms

Embarrassment about asking a doctor for attention

Sense of anger if a doctor doesn't pay enough attention to me

Difficulty recognizing opportunities or slow to react to them

Tendency to be oversolicitous of people in my care, such as children or subordinates at work

SPIRITUAL BELIEFS

Sense that God doesn't care about my needs

Sense that God is annoyed by my needs

Next, give at least one example in your journal of a specific instance of your experience of any characteristics you have listed.

Example

Difficulty Receiving Care Giving from Others: Last winter when I had to stay in bed with the flu, I felt either embarrassed, irritated, or both whenever my wife came into the bedroom to check on me, or to bring me juice or medicine.

Childhood Memories

You may have an actual memory of your care givers nurturing you. You may also get in touch with a point of reference to which you can compare this actual memory. This point of reference is the image of perfect parenting induced by the activation of the inner contact point and toward which we are driven with deep inner longing. The gap between the actual memory and the point of reference is the experience of neglect.

Following are guidelines for writing in your journal about what you can remember of how your parents and other care givers responded to your need for nurture.

Before You Begin

Spend a brief moment relaxing. Put aside whatever current concerns you have, and pray for the capacity to recall what you are ready to remember about your childhood. Don't worry if there are few or no memories about this section. If you haven't done much work with your memories, they may come slowly. Remember that patience and attentiveness toward yourself in this process are the specific attitudes that heal childhood neglect. In addition, if your experience of neglect was not as intense as your experience of enmeshment, abuse, or abandonment, there may be less to remember.

Memory Time

Read the following, then try to remember how your care givers responded to your neediness and dependence. For example, when you asked for a glass of water, a bedtime story, or a hug (could you ask for a hug?), how did your parents respond? When you asked for attention, to feel special, or to have your tastes honored or ideas listened to, what was their response? Perhaps their response was one of these (use this list to help prompt your memory for the responses of your parents):

> *Did my care givers*
>
> 1. ignore me?
> 2. consider me an imposition on their already exhausted condition?
> 3. tell me I was ungrateful, lazy, unresourceful, or insensitive and that I should know better than to bother her or him?
> 4. tell me I was selfish or sinful?
> 5. somehow give me the message that asking for attention, help, guidance, or money was an imposition and that I had to pay it back?

It may be that you now have difficulty remembering things distinctly, as though you had few memorable reactions. Perhaps one or more of the following is true.

- I had few attachments to anything or anyone.
- I was "in a fog" during most of my childhood.
- I have few or no memories of all or parts of my childhood.

Journal Guidelines

Describe in your journal your memories about the responses of each of the following to your neediness and dependence:

1. Your father
2. Your mother
3. Any other care givers (give name and care-giving relationship to you)

Example

Mrs. Jenkins, My Third Grade Teacher: When I asked her to explain an arithmetic problem to me, she told me I needed to pay better attention to the explanations she gave the entire class, because there were too many students for her to have time to explain things to each person individually.

NOTES

1. J. B. Watson and R. Rayner, "Conditioned Emotional Reactions," *Journal of Experimental Psychology,* 1920, 3: 1–14.
2. Carol Roberts, "The Wounded Feeling Function and Dependency Behaviors." Presentation at Journey into Wholeness Conference, Hendersonville, NC, Nov. 9–13, 1987.

8

Experiences of Enmeshment

When we have experienced enmeshment in childhood, two characteristics seem to be prevalent: (1) difficulty with personal choices, and (2) projection.

Choices: When enmeshment has occurred, we experience difficulty making choices, or even knowing that we have preferences in certain areas of our lives. The ability to have preferences is directly related to establishing healthy boundaries.

Pia Mellody says a boundary is two things: (1) an invisible, permeable buffer that we place between us and someone else's reality coming at us, protecting us from being injured or overwhelmed by the other person's reality and keeping our reality from injuring or overpowering others, and (2) an invisible envelope within which we develop our individual selves.[1]

Many kinds of boundaries affect our choice making. A physical boundary involves how close we allow others to come to us, how we allow them to touch us, and so forth. A sexual boundary involves when, where, with whom, and how we are sexual. An emotional boundary allows us to recognize when another person's emotions are about that person and not us. An intellectual boundary gives us the ability to choose our own ideas and opinions, and to make decisions and solve problems our own way. A spiritual boundary allows us to have our own spiritual experience without others telling us how it has to fit certain ecclesiastical or dogmatic categories (for our own good, of course).

There is, unfortunately, spiritual enmeshment. Sometimes people who really love the church actually leave it because they feel so enmeshed. They do this because they need the space to get validation for their own spiritual experience. Bill W., cofounder of Alcoholics Anonymous, seems to have been an example of such a person. He was so wary of churches because of his own past history with them that he kept saying that A.A. is a spiritual program—not religious but spiritual. It seems to us that what he meant basically was that A.A. is very focused on a relationship with God but is not a church.

Projection: Along with problems around choice making comes the tendency to project onto others what is actually within ourselves. When the boundary or distinction between ourselves and someone else is not clear to us, we are likely to think that what is going on with us is really going on with the other person. Projection occurs when we attribute to someone else something that is actually going on within us that we are unwilling to face. For example, Barry is angry when his girlfriend, Sue, is late. But he sees himself as "too good a person" to be angry, so he accuses Sue of being angry in reaction to his criticism. Sue begins insisting she is not angry, which, in Barry's mind, only betrays her irritation.

As children, we are mentally egocentric. We see events from our point of view only and cannot imagine them from anyone else's point of view. After about age six, we develop the mental capacity to "de-center" and can appreciate the viewpoints of others. This lays the foundation, mentally at least, for mutuality in relationships. However, our ability to de-center may be impaired if we are enmeshed by other family members at a young age. Because *we* do not experience ourselves as having an independent viewpoint (with independent feelings), we have difficulty recognizing that others have this experience or need it. If family members have projected their "reality" onto us, we cannot discover where they end and we begin, and we do not develop healthy boundaries. If we do not develop healthy boundaries and thus remain stuck in childhood egocentrism, we are likely to enmesh with other people when we relate to them, seeing them as extensions of ourselves.

We can say, then, that the experience of childhood enmeshment drives the process of projection. As we will demonstrate, we can project negative (shadow side) or positive (growth edge) qualities from ourselves onto others. As long as we stay in our projection, we avoid realizing that these potentials actually lie within us.

We can learn to recognize that we are projecting by tuning in whenever we exhibit either of two forms of response to a person or event. One response is irritation or anger at one or more disagreeable characteristics or traits we perceive in someone else. The aspect of ourselves being projected in these instances is referred to as our shadow side. The other response we may have when we are projecting is a strong positive attraction for someone, often a romantic or sexual attraction. The aspect of ourselves being projected is often either a *growth area* within ourselves or a *corrective action* we need to take in our lives. An example of the need for a corrective action being projected is when someone finds a defiant leather-jacketed motorcyclist curiously attractive. The attraction may indicate that the person needs to develop his or her own assertiveness or independence.

The goal of the second stage of our childhood development after integrating trust and mistrust is to integrate *autonomy with doubt and shame.* Autonomy comes from the activation of our longing for perfect companionship and emotional development. As we begin to develop relationships with others in a less-than-perfect environment, and try to gain awareness of ourselves as separate entities from other people, our care givers may overrun our boundaries. If this happens, doubt and shame enter the picture.

Not completing this integration can lead to becoming stuck at one or the other of the two stances. Developing only autonomy leads to developing solid walls of independence instead of healthy boundaries. We are on our own and set up walls to keep others out. With solid walls, we are unable to relate to others, primarily because we are not sensitized to the point of view of others and therefore have no way to negotiate a relationship. On the other hand, developing only shame and doubt leads to the condition of having no boundaries, or damaged ones, which leaves us too vulnerable to others to have healthy relationships. Or we may jump back and forth between having walls and no boundaries, unable to integrate the two into healthy boundaries.

When we enter the second stage of childhood development and growth, our dual experience with autonomy, coming from our inner longing, and with shame and doubt, coming from our outer experiences in our environment, calls forth another style of learning called *social learning.*[2] Social learning is one of the reasons it is good for our boundaries to be permeable. We can acquire an entire range of complex responses through modeling, as we observe someone else's behavior instead of having to learn in the more piecemeal style of classical conditioning. A personal relationship becomes the vehicle for acquiring these new responses quickly rather than having to learn them a bit at a time by interacting with a preexisting structure, as we did through the classical conditioning method of learning.

A certain amount of permeability in our boundaries is healthy and helpful. We can protect ourselves in relationships by *making sound choices* from within healthy boundaries rather than operating from behind solid walls or with no boundaries at all. The problem we need to address is being *impressionable* to the point that we exclude our own reality in favor of another's. As we address the problem of being too susceptible, however, we must try not to go too far and lose sight of the benefit of this capacity in the first place.

Recovery from each form of childhood injury evidently includes making use of the particular learning style that was operating when we were injured. For those of us who experienced enmeshment in childhood, two things are important: (1) developing the ability to make choices around each area of the self (physical, sexual, emotional, intellectual, spiritual) and (2) choosing healthy recovering people to model ourselves after. In the Twelve-Step recovery process, the concept of having a sponsor fits this idea of learning by modeling. In selecting a sponsor, we can look for someone who has what we want in terms of healthy thinking, emotions, behavior, and spirituality.

Enmeshment creates a gap between our yearning for a perfect learning relationship and the reality of what happened to us in our family of origin when we were treated as extensions of our parents. Our care givers often redirect our choices and actions—perhaps in the name of good taste and education—but in a way that destroys our sense of choice. It is not so much the adjustments we made that are the problem, although they sometimes are dysfunctional also, but rather the attitude about relationships that we developed. We experience injury when our care givers give us the message that fulfilling relationships involve conforming to the needs and reality of *another* person, and disregarding *our own* needs and reality.

If we did not get enough space to develop *our own identity* as a child, we are set up to have the expectation that someone else is going to direct us in the areas that we ought to deal with ourselves. If we find a relationship with a person who will not take over and give us the identity we lack in ourselves, we may feel frustrated or disappointed. If we find a relationship with a person who does take over our lives, we may have a sense of familiarity and security at first, but then feel resentment if the person doesn't do it "right," and also feel helpless, and hopeless, and trapped.

When enough people have let us down, we may attempt to turn away from the yearning itself or smother the need in some way. We ourselves can't satisfy it, and we know that no one else can make our life choices for us. So the hunger goes on, and we try to ignore it or grimly endure it.

Carol Roberts's work with patients recovering from chemical dependency, referred to in chapter 7, revealed that one of the effects desired from drugs was euphoria, getting high. People who have experienced enmeshment may tend to take drugs for their euphoric effect because the drugs helped them get in touch with their own reality by exaggerating it. They experience a temporary loss of boundaries and a pleasurable fusion with other people. But eventually the harmful consequences of these drugs cancel out the euphoria. The drugs suppress or misdirect the deep yearning for a perfect relationship that respects boundaries, choices, and personal development. Drug use specifically erodes the capacity for relationships with other people, because the drug user's primary emotional relationship is with the drug, not with other human beings.

Roberts suggests that the same pleasurable effect from the euphoric drug may be achieved more gradually by participating in some of these activities: exercise, appropriate sex, relaxation, listening to music, or having fun.[3] These healthier endeavors may *fill the inner hunger that drove the person toward the drug* in the first place.

In our hearts, we yearn for a perfect relationship with someone who will relate to us without trying to take over our lives, who will respect and honor our choices and call us into our own identity. Something within our very souls drives us to seek such a perfect relationship in our lives. Entering recovery and facing our need to make our own choices can be frightening and painful because we get in touch with the feelings of betrayal about having learned unhealthy approaches to life and relationships from inadequate care givers.

Adult Characteristics

The following list cites typical characteristics of adult behavior in people who experienced enmeshment from care givers in childhood. Read through the list and specify in your journal any that pertain to you, or any other characteristics that seem to you to relate to any enmeshment experiences:

DIFFICULTY MAKING CHOICES

Often unable to say no to unreasonable requests of superiors or co-workers

Difficulty knowing preferences, especially when someone else's feelings will be hurt by my choice

Difficulty or fear of getting angry when someone dominates me or violates my rights

Unable/unwilling to share feelings which might threaten a relationship

Often agree too quickly with authorities, parents, supervisors, the church

Tendency to idealize or imitate boss or co-workers instead of exploring my own way of doing things

PROJECTION

Strong reaction to faults in others; difficulty recognizing these potentials within me

Tendency to justify or take side of person who has overrun me

Overinvolvement in the emotions of others (when someone close to me hurts, I hurt, even though situation is not about me)

Oversensitivity to rejection or criticism

Tendency to sexualize work relationships

Preoccupation about someone else much of the time

SPIRITUAL BELIEFS

Sense that God is one who invades my privacy, controls/judges my free choice, or imposes moral "answers" on me even before I ask the question

Sense that God probably doesn't love me in my independent moral decisions, especially in complicated areas where there are no clear-cut answers

Next, give one or more examples in your journal of specific instances of your experience of any items you have listed.

Example

Oversensitivity to Rejection or Criticism: My boss made a request that I change the way I write up the budget for my department. I was so hurt and angry that I had to hurry back to my office, close and lock the door, and cry for ten minutes. It was hard to look him in the eye when I gave him the budget in the format he wanted.

Childhood Memories

We may have an actual memory of our parents giving us the space within which to develop some aspects of ourselves, and other memories of times when they did not. The gap between the actual parenting we received and our longing for perfect companionship that allows emotional growth is what we call the experience of enmeshment.

Following are guidelines for writing in your journal about what you can remember of how your parents and other care givers treated your individuality.

Before You Begin

Spend a brief moment relaxing. Put aside whatever current concerns you have, and pray for the capacity to recall what you are ready to remember about your childhood. Don't worry if you have only a few memories about this section, or even none at all. Remember, if you haven't done much work with your memories, they may come slowly. In addition, if the experience of enmeshment was not as intense as your experience of neglect, abuse, or abandonment, there may be less to remember here.

Memory Time

Read the following list and try to remember the way your parents and other care givers dealt with your individuality:

Did my care givers

1. respect my need for privacy?
2. respect my need for emotional independence?
3. permit me to express ideas or opinions that were different from theirs?
4. show respect for my ideas or opinions that were different from theirs?
5. permit me to express and enact spiritual beliefs that were different from theirs?
6. permit me to openly disagree with them without feelings being hurt?
7. give me chances to make my own choices appropriate with my stage of maturity rather than having to please them by conforming to their expectations? Areas to consider: clothing, food, hobbies, friends, schedule, boyfriends/girlfriends, schoolwork, employment, religious practice.

Journaling Guidelines

Describe in your journal your memories about how each of the following treated your individuality:

1. Your father
2. Your mother
3. Other care givers (give name and care-giving relationship to you)

Example

My mother taught me how to fold the bathroom towels from the dryer a certain way to fit on the narrow shelf in the linen closet. When I discovered another way to fold them that would still fit the shelf but required less adjustment when we got them out to put on the towel bars, she got upset and made me refold the towels, saying I hadn't done it right.

NOTES

1. Pia Mellody, with Andrea Wells Miller and J. Keith Miller, *Facing Codependence* (San Francisco: Harper San Francisco, 1989).
2. A. Bandura and R. Walters, *Social Learning and Personality Development* (New York: Rinehart and Winston, 1963).
3. Carol Roberts, "The Wounded Feeling Function and Dependency Behaviors." Presentation at Journey into Wholeness Conference, Hendersonville, NC, Nov. 9–13, 1987.

9

Experiences of Abuse

On the surface the core problem resulting from childhood abuse seems to be that the child victim might become an offender as an adult. But the underlying principal issue for the child may actually be having enough freedom or a safe enough place to do his or her trial-and-error exploration of the environment; this is the principal way the child learns from experience. In fact, our mistakes are what teach us the most about our individuality, our unique style. The experience of abuse in childhood leads to a loss of personal power that jeopardizes our sense of safety and freedom. We conclude that the world is not a safe place to be, and thus it is dangerous to venture out and try things, to behave powerfully and uniquely as an individual. Consequently, we may abuse our power with those whom we perceive to be weaker than ourselves, or cower before those we think are stronger.

How we get things done or properly use our power is based on what we learned to do as children to survive. If people physically abused us as children for our faults or mistakes or for our natural way of being—imperfect, immature children—it's pretty hard to feel safe as an adult, especially in relationship with others. The message received by the child is that the world is not safe outside or inside the self.

We react as adults to this loss of safety and freedom with a range of responses. On one end of the range, we may become rebellious or too aggressive in our need to create a safe, free environment for ourselves. We may be too argumentative, belligerent, and at times even violent. This attitude is sometimes called a rebellious/defiant stance. On the other end of the range, we may attempt to be always good or perfect, approaching life from a defensive stance, giving up our freedom and hoping to create safety for ourselves by trying not to cause any reasons for others to abuse us.

Our experience of our care givers as they misuse power creates a gap between what our hearts long for in terms of proficiency and personal power and what we actually learn. If our natural desire to explore our environment is met by frequent and severe punishment and trauma, our natural capacity for initiative and desire to explore our world and learn by our own experience gets quashed.

We may develop unrealistic expectations about how others ought to respond to us. For example, we might mistakenly interpret independent behavior of others as abusive. Also, we may mistakenly think that our abuse toward others is only the way we "stand up for ourselves."

When enough painful consequences have occurred in relationships with others because of our inability to properly use our power, we may attempt to turn away from the natural desire for proficiency and try to ignore it. We experience discomfort as we try to live with this unmet need, knowing that no one can give us a sense of safety and freedom all the time. The discomfort continues as we use inept methods of coping with others and with life.

The goal of the third stage in childhood development, after integrating autonomy with doubt and shame, is to integrate *initiative* with *guilt*. Initiative is linked to the activation of our longing for perfect power and freedom. As we work with this longing in the the not so perfect world, we eventually transgress certain standards of behavior, either our own or that of our care givers. Guilt stems from this.

If we are unable to integrate initiative with guilt and get stuck at one of the two positions, we carry certain difficulties into adulthood with us. Developing only initiative leads us toward being too rebellious, a maverick. Developing only guilt leads us toward being perfectionistic and inhibited. Or we may flip-flop back and forth, not integrating the opposites, living in extremes and not moving forward developmentally.

The third stage of growth and development in our childhood in which we deal with both our inner initiative drive and the outer experiences of guilt, calls forth a third learning style, described as *operant conditioning*.[1] A common illustration of how operant conditioning works is that of a white rat searching for a lever that, when pressed, delivers a food pellet. The rat explores its environment, trying various behaviors, until it gets a reward. By this trial-and-error process, the rat's behavior is conditioned by the rewards or the lack of rewards it receives.

In *operant conditioning,* the child initiates behavior to get places, to look at things, and to draw conclusions from exploratory experience.

A sense of stimulation and heightened behavioral freedom was one of the effects sought after by drug users, according to the observations of Carol Roberts, mentioned in chapter 7. People who experienced childhood abuse may often seek drugs with a stimulant effect, giving them an energetic, excited, empowered feeling. Taking stimulants reflects the misdirected yearning for perfect power and freedom. But sooner or later, the harmful consequences of these drugs counteract whatever sense of stimulation or empowerment they provided.

Roberts suggests that a person might fill this need by participating in some of these activities: sports, high-risk activities, visits to amusement parks, skydiving, skiing, or seeing scary movies. Persons may be able to *fill the inner hunger that drove the person toward the drug* in the first place by engaging in these activities.[2]

Creating an appropriate sense of safety and freedom as an adult is the challenge for recovering from the experience of abuse in childhood. Our hearts yearn for power and freedom and yet our care givers demonstrated an improper use of their power toward us. Becoming aware of the gap between our heart's yearning and the actual care giver's modeling of power can be rather frightening, because we become more consciously aware of our lack of safety and our deprivation of freedom. The new awareness can also be painful as we realize that what we thought were reasonable ways of negotiating, having arguments, or expressing anger may actually be abusive to others.

Adult Characteristics

Some of the typical adult behaviors of people who experienced abuse from care givers in childhood appear in the following list. Read the list and write in your journal any that pertain to you, or any others that seem to you to relate to any form of abuse:

REBELLIOUS/DEFIANT

Tendency to dismiss legitimate requests made by authority figures
Tendency to mock, make fun of, or discredit authority figures
Tendency to resort to explosive emotions to fight for my rights
Tendency to resort to physical force to get my way or to express anger
Tendency to be argumentative; strong desire to win at all costs
Difficulty seeing the other person's point of view

GOOD/PERFECT

Overconforming, fears of being hurt if I do not "give in"
Lack of initiative, excessive need for explicit instructions

Often allow others to touch me in painful ways at home or at work

Difficulty standing up for my own rights, difficulty responding with appropriate assertiveness

Fear or concern that someone in authority will use power irrationally or excessively against me in any of the following ways:

- Economically (boss, creditor, loan officer at a bank)
- Physically (police, intimidating neighbor)
- Spiritually (public shaming, intimidation, or rejection by a religious authority)

SPIRITUAL BELIEFS

Sense of God as self-serving and avenging

Belief that God will actively and severely punish me for my sins

Belief that God must be appeased or I will be made to suffer for my faults, mistakes, sins

Next, give one or more examples in your journal of specific instances of your experience of any items you have listed.

Example

Difficulty Standing Up for My Own Rights with Appropriate Assertiveness: Last month I told my former college roommate, who lives in Massachusetts, that I needed to postpone her trip to my house for two weeks so I could heal from some oral surgery that I was having. She responded by telling me not to worry, I would probably be all right, and then went on to talk about getting her airline tickets for the trip. Instead of telling her firmly not to come, I just sighed and thought, "Oh well, I tried," and allowed her to visit while I was still having pain from the surgery.

Childhood Memories

We may have actual memories of physical contact with our care givers that was nurturing, such as hugs at bedtime or sitting snuggled up with a parent while watching television. We may also have memories of physical contact that didn't feel good, or no memories at all of anybody touching anybody in the family. There may have been instances when our care givers used their power for our benefit (to protect us from an outside danger or to teach us in a positive way), and instances when they misused their power in our relationship or did not protect us. The gap between the actual experiences of parental power and the longing for experiences of appropriate power and freedom, is the experience of abuse.

Following are guidelines for writing in your journal about what you can remember of how your parents and other care givers used their power in their relationship with you.

Before You Begin

Spend a brief moment relaxing. Put aside whatever current concerns you have, and pray for the capacity to recall what you are ready to remember about your childhood. Don't worry if your memories about abuse are few or nonexistent. If you haven't done much work with your memories, such memories may come slowly. If the experience of abuse was not as intense as your experience of neglect, enmeshment, or abandonment, there may be less to remember here.

Memory Time

Read the following and try to remember any ways your parents or other care givers misused their power with you.

Did my care givers

1. hurt me physically or sexually?
2. physically punish me? If so, what were the punishments?
3. touch me in a way that was either painful or shaming?
4. have explosive emotions such as rage or disruptive anxiety over anything about me: my behavior, mistakes, looks, and so on?
5. aggressively use me to meet their needs? (For example, insisting that a daughter take modeling lessons and enter pageants beginning in the second grade, over her protests, because the mother enjoyed being in the world of beauty pageants.)

Journaling Guidelines

Describe in your journal your memories about how each of the following care givers used his or her power over you in areas just described or in other areas that relate to the abuse of power:

1. Your father
2. Your mother
3. Other care givers (give name and care-giving relationship to you)

Example

My father insisted that I play Little League even though I wasn't very coordinated. It seemed to me that he needed me to be on a team so he could enjoy camaraderie with the other fathers, or perhaps he needed me to be an athlete to prove he was a masculine father.

NOTES

1. B. F. Skinner, *The Technology of Teaching* (New York: Appleton-Century Crofts, 1968).
2. Carol Roberts, "The Wounded Feeling Function and Dependency Behaviors." Presentation at Journey into Wholeness Conference, Hendersonville, NC, Nov. 9–13, 1987.

10

Experiences of Abandonment

When we have experienced abandonment in childhood, the primary difficulty seems to be dealing with losses as adults. In fact, a person who has experienced either traumatic changes or separation from a care giver seems to respond in one of two ways: (1) tries to avoid going through the necessary losses of life, or (2) reacts to them as crippling or unfair.

Losses are necessary to growth and are a natural part of life. They are part of the process of making transitions from one life stage to another or from one context to another. The law of growth involves surrendering precisely our principal strength in order to move on to the next growth level, and yet making a transition might seem almost like death itself for a person who has experienced abandonment in childhood.

The goal of the fourth stage of childhood development, after integrating initiative with guilt, is to integrate *industry* with *inferiority*. The deep longing for perfect meaning and purpose ignites our desire for competence, our industrial energies. As we face various transitions in less-than-perfect settings, we encounter situational difficulties. Our first feelings of inferiority occur.

If this integration is not accomplished, we become frozen at one side or the other. Being frozen at the industry position leads us toward megalomania, a sense that our own ideas and models are greater than the world's. Being frozen at the inferiority position leads us toward a sense of the world being so overwhelming and chaotic that we cannot figure it out.

When we arrive at a fourth stage of growth and development in childhood, our struggle with dual experience from our inner longing and our outer difficulties in less-than-perfect surroundings calls forth a style of learning described as *cognitive modeling*.[1, 2] This involves organizing our insights and perceptions that can transfer from one environment or situation to another. Such learning includes developing internal mental models of reality and the ability to abstract from one environment the principles that are useful in a new context.

For example, Robert Bolles, in his book *What Color Is Your Parachute?*, helped people draw from their previous job experiences what he called transferable job skills. He did this because, when asked what they've done before, most people list the specific things they did in a specific environment for a specific boss. Bolles taught people to step back mentally from the specifics and generalize their job skills into more abstract abilities such as organizing, categorizing, recording, or information processing, so they could take what they had learned and apply it to a number of contexts.

The fourth contact point activated during childhood—the longing for meaning and perspective—is the "mapmaker," model builder, and systems maintainer. The energy resulting from the awakening of this longing keeps everything else going because it's the master regulator operating within us. But to be most effective, it has to be generalized enough to apply to a number of environments. Every time we change environments, we learn a little more about what's essential. After making a transition, we may realize that what we thought was a general truth about reality was actually only a specific instance of something. This has implications for our faith, because it seems we are being led by God surely and slowly to a deeper notion of what reality is. It's as if God tells us, "That's not all of it. There is more to this than you see right now."

As adults, the level of difficulty we have negotiating losses seems to be related to how intense our childhood abandonment experiences were. As a result of these experiences of abandonment, we may have an obsessive need to control what is going on so that we can understand it. On the other hand, however, we may give up and sink into depression and passivity, believing there is no use trying to make sense of our seemingly chaotic world.

The result is that we are likely to react negatively to changes in our lives, resisting them from a deep level. Changes such as moving away from home for the first time, the loss of privacy because of living with a roommate, a mother's experience of the last child leaving home, the loss of a job, bankruptcy, a robbery, one's own body aging, divorce, or the death of a friend or family member can seem like ultimate tragedy to one who has experienced childhood abandonment.

Such difficulty with loss can translate into a specific effect desired from drugs, called an *hallucinatory* effect, according to Carol Roberts's work with recovering addicts, cited in chapter 7. Those who experienced childhood abandonment may feel inclined to take drugs for their hallucinogenic effect, that is, a kind of relief from coping with the hard realities of losses and change, and an escape to a different reality. The alternate realities have their own problems however, and the capacity to create and maintain a meaningful life is weakened by escapism. Escape to a different reality through hallucinogenic drugs is not an effective solution to the yearning for understanding and perspective.

For people who seek a hallucinatory effect, Roberts suggests participating in some of these activities: practicing meditation, going to church, reading science fiction, practicing yoga, or rebirthing.[3] These activities are healthy alternatives to drugs and may help *fill the inner hunger that drove the person toward the drug* in the first place.

Coming to terms with changes and losses as a natural part of life can be painful and frightening for a person who has experienced childhood abandonment. An image Jesus used to talk about coming to terms with painful change is that of a woman in labor:

> A woman giving birth to a child has pain because her time has come but when her baby is born she forgets the anguish because of her joy that a child is born into the world. (John 16:21)

Our various contexts and stages of life are like pregnancy. We don't remain pregnant forever. The end of each stage may involve great pain and travail like a pregnancy. But when we get through the pain to the next stage or context, we forget the pain and marvel at the new life.

God's way of leading us through growth is evidently to peel off deeper and deeper layers of our superficial self, who we think we are, like the husk being peeled off the kernel of grain. At such times, we receive God's invitation to go even deeper into our inner selves.

Adult Characteristics

Typical characteristics of adult behavior of people who experienced abandonment (constant or frequent separation) from care givers in childhood are included in the following list. Read through the list and write in your journal any that pertain to you, or any others that seem to you to be connected to experiences of abandonment:

DEALING WITH LOSS

Sense of life as meaningless or hopeless, and yearning to escape from it

Obsessive need to control myself, others, my environment in my home, at work, in relationships

Fear of exposure as inadequate or incompetent, as not knowing
what I'm supposed to know at work or in social settings

Tendency toward depression

Difficulty thinking and acting efficiently to work productively

Tendency to react to independent behavior of others (such as father,
mother, siblings, friends, co-workers, sexual partner, children)
as if I have been abandoned

Sense that meaning has gone out of my life and I have lost my
center because someone has left me or let me down

Tendency to feel abandoned by the leadership or programs of
organizations I am associated with, such as a church,
workplace, social group (even a recovery group), or a country

Sense of confusion or of being overwhelmed in new situations, as
though I don't know what to do

SPIRITUAL BELIEFS

Sense that God has abandoned me

Sense that God began the world but then went away

Difficulty opening myself to new ideas of God, based on my life
experience

Next, give one or more examples in your journal of specific instances of your
experience of any items you have listed.

Example

*Fear of Being Revealed as Incompetent, as Not Knowing What I'm Supposed to Do
in Social Settings:* I spent four hours last Saturday afternoon trying on clothes
in an attempt to decide what to wear to a friend's wedding. Although I have
plenty of clothes, everything seemed either too dressy, too flashy, or too plain. Although people were polite to me at the reception, I just knew they were thinking how stupid I looked and that I didn't know how to dress for an evening
wedding.

Childhood Memories

We may have memories of our care givers being present for us, giving us the time,
attention, and direction we needed. Or we may have memories of times when
they were not present for us because of circumstances beyond their control
such as illness, death, or dysfunctional problems such as addictions. The gap

between the amount of attention we received and the image planted in our souls by the activation of our longing for meaning and perspective, we call the experience of abandonment.

Before You Begin

Spend a brief moment relaxing. Put aside whatever current concerns you have, and pray for the capacity to recall what you can about your childhood. Don't worry if you have few or no memories of any abandonment experiences. Remember, if you haven't done much work with your memories, they may come slowly. In addition, if your experience of abandonment was not as intense as your experience of neglect, enmeshment, or abuse, there may be less to remember here than in other sections.

Memory Time

Read the following and try to remember any ways you may have experienced a sense of loss or separation from parents or other care givers.

Did my care givers

1. separate me often or for a long time from primary family members, such as mother, father, siblings, or other family members?
2. threaten me with abandonment as a way of controlling my behavior?
3. move frequently so that I often lost connections with neighborhoods and friends?
4. abandon me through their work or pastimes, such as long hunting trips, military assignments, solitary hobbies, or social events outside the family?
5. show up for significant events in my life?
6. give me enough time and attention for me to identify with them as part of my heritage?
7. expect me to figure out how to do most things on my own?

Do I

8. have any friends from my childhood?
9. feel that I did not fit in with the rest of my family?

Journaling Guidelines

Describe in your journal your memories about your experience with each of the following care givers concerning the questions just listed:

1. Your father
2. Your mother
3. Other care givers (give name and care-giving relationship to you)

Example

Moved Frequently so that I Lost Contact with Neighborhoods and Friends: My father was in the military. We moved often so I don't have any childhood friends. When I recently told my daughter about leaving my horse, Flame, in Addis Ababa, Ethiopia, I wept, even now as an adult. I still carry the pain of knowing that place would never be the same even if I could go back because the people I knew were also in the military and they would be gone.

NOTES

1. E. C. Tolman, "Cognitive Maps in Rats and Men," *Psychological Review,* 1948, *55,* 189–208.
2. J. Bruner, *Toward a Theory of Instruction* (Cambridge, MA: Belknap Press of Harvard Univ. Press, 1966).
3. Carol Roberts, "The Wounded Feeling Function and Dependency Behaviors." Presentation at Journey into Wholeness Conference, Hendersonville, NC, Nov. 9–13, 1987.

Part III

Spiritual Healing

11

Directing Our Inner
Longing to God

One of the most important things that has been reemphasized by the recovery community is that only a program of spiritual recovery will answer the deepest yearnings in people's hearts. Many people who simply learn better coping skills often relapse. Spiritual recovery can be very effective for a problem that is spiritual at root.

Now we are ready to embark on a spiritual recovery journey. We have gained new sensitivity to the existence of deep internal longings within us and how they have been misdirected. We have journaled about the specific ways they have been steered off course—and the problems we have experienced in our own individual lives as a result.

The original gift of these contact points is still available to us. We can harness these profound internal energies triggered during childhood, even though they are now misdirected, and use them for a beneficial purpose in our recovery. With the information we have gained about ourselves and the forms of injury we experienced in childhood, we can begin the process of redirecting, repairing, and restoring these energies toward deeper spiritual connections with God.

Spiritual Connections Give Us Greater Capacity to Live

From our connection to God, we receive release from whatever adult symptoms we experience as a result of our encounters with neglect, enmeshment, abuse, and abandonment. As we are emptied of the aftermath of these childhood injuries, we are filled with the nurture, solace, sensitivity, and maturity God intended us to have. Out of this fullness we derive a healthier capacity for discerning *when* to be of help to others and when to refrain because of our own lack of resources, trusting that when we need to refrain, God can and will find a solution for the other person. We can learn how to allow God both to provide the solace and nurture *we need* and to handle the job of finding the appropriate source of the solace and nurture both for ourselves and for others, when appropriate. In this way, God can fill us with resources so that our lives overflow toward others out of fullness.

We need to be a well, not a pipe. Water flows through a pipe for people, but after it has flowed through, the pipe itself is empty. But a well overflows from its fullness, which comes from the depths (in this case, our contact points), and, after "water" is given to others, the well is still full. For example, Jesus said, "But whoever drinks the water I give him will never be thirsty; no, the water I give shall become *a fountain within him*, leaping up to provide eternal life [italics ours]" (John 4:13–14).

In addition, we can more clearly perceive *how* to be of help to others without enmeshing with them or ab-using our power with regard to their lives. The stronger our spiritual connections, the greater our level of surrender and trust in God. This surrender brings a life-enhancing joy to our relationships with others, and reduces the chance of our experiencing these relationships as draining burdens or painful circumstance to be endured.

The Bible

The Bible tells us how God intended for us to relate to God and others in a healthy way. The Scriptures tell us how to live so that we can be whole and therefore available for each other without being overwhelmed or burned out, and without taking over God's role in our own or someone else's life.

There is more than one approach to using Scripture to inform our lives.[1] With a historical approach, we look at Scripture as a record of salvation history. With a moral approach, we can find in the Bible a moral guideline for behavior and behavior change. The anagogical, or future-oriented, approach to Scripture points out where people are headed in terms of another realm, one of full realization of relationship with God. Another approach to Bible stories is allegorical interpretation, in which we consider that the stories are an analogy of our personal spiritual situation—in which the characters in the story represent facets of our psychological makeup. When viewed this way, many biblical parables depict journeys toward psychological healing. By using allegorical interpretation, we will look at several biblical stories that help us understand the four wounded and misdirected aspects in ourselves.

RECOVERING CONNECTIONS

Writers such as John Sanford, who examined the parables in his book *The Kingdom Within,* and Helen Luke, who wrote *Myth and Symbolism in the Bible and Literature,* are renewing the tradition of an allegorical way of looking at parables. Actually, this tradition has existed since the earliest centuries of Christianity. It reveals in a different way the wisdom of these biblical images that pull us into a deeper reality. These biblical stories give us images that speak the symbolic language of the deep unconscious, the language of the soul.

Gospels: We will examine some of the things Jesus taught in the Gospels about how to live in recovery with our deepest internal energies directed toward God. The four Gospels, taken together, give us a pattern of wholeness. Within Eastern religions, such as Buddhism, one finds mandalas, graphic symbolic patterns depicting four fundamental dimensions of human experience that, when joined together, represent wholeness. Implied in a mandala is the idea that if any one of the four aspects is omitted, wholeness cannot exist. Mandalas are often used as focal points by which people meditate about wholeness. Everyday examples of mandalas are the four directions of the compass and the four seasons, representing a totality of place and time.

Many people think that only religions of the East emphasize this wisdom about mandalas and wholeness, but the Christian tradition also reflects this wisdom. For instance, the cross itself has four points, each end of the two crossed beams. Another reflection of a mandala is found in the four Gospels. They are like a living mandala of Jesus Christ. It is not surprising that these four (not five or three) were adopted by the whole Christian community. These four sides of the Christ story speak to us about healing in four dimensions. There is a particular journey of healing in each of the four Gospels that seems to speak to each of the four forms of injury: Matthew speaks to neglect, Luke speaks to enmeshment, Mark speaks to abuse, and John speaks to abandonment.

But if anyone focuses on just one aspect, one gospel truth, he or she may quickly move away from the *whole* message of Christianity. And in the same way, if we focus on healing from just one aspect of childhood injury, we deprive ourselves of the wholeness we can find in spiritual recovery.

Parables and Other Stories: By definition, a parable is a story that has a deeper meaning.[2] Each recovery chapter includes one or more parables or other stories from the Bible dealing with the relevant form of injury, drawing out the message of healing contained in the story.

Stories are important for psychological healing. The Bible is richly laced with stories. An allegorical approach to Scripture can be quite helpful for seeing the tale of the journey of the human soul, how each one of us goes through things, in our story, our recovery, our journey. We know that as a species we don't like to get explicit requests for change. We human beings typically resist rules. We have a wonderful, yet dangerous, need to do it our way. Stories allow us to see and accept the need for change and for following structured guidelines for living, and point the way to what changes are needed, but they allow us to make our own individual application.

Growth involves sacrifice, a certain kind of "death" in order to move into new life. We've seen examples of this paradox in Erik Erikson's theory of development. How do you communicate a paradox to people? It can't be done easily with explicit explanations of rules that we already understand and categories and other obvious left-brain things. We evidently need a different level of communication to understand paradoxical reality. Approaching the Bible allegorically can bypass our human resistance through symbols that connect us to ever deeper levels of understanding, allowing us to experience the paradoxical union of opposites. Instead of the paradox being forced on us, we find ourselves in the middle of it. (For example, I am the robbed man being helped by the accursed Samaritan.) And because the union of opposites and paradoxes is apparently a universal law of growth, stories are one of the best ways to talk about spiritual growth, about recovery. This may be why sharing our *story* in small groups can turn out to be the most helpful information leading to growth for others in the group.

Stories About the Spiritual Recovery Journey

In our time, people who get together to share amazing stories about spiritual connections and their impact on ordinary lives aren't found in church classrooms as much as one would expect. Rather such people gather in gyms, they gather in church cafeterias or basements, office spaces, or other ordinary places. They sit down and say, "Hi, my name is Bill, and I'm an alcoholic"—or a codependent or something else. Then they tell their stories, describing real-life events in which they experience something greater than their conscious ego at work in themselves, moving them toward recovery.

The promise of science—and "scientific" psychology—to give us deep answers to life has fallen on hard times. By contrast, the current interest in learning about myths offers answers to our deep need for stories relevant to our longings. Such stories carry us in their wisdom, pointing out the path of this deep growth and giving us some markers to follow as we go deeper into our unconscious.

Recovery can be viewed in two ways: (1) the overall dynamic of the spiritual recovery process, and (2) specific issues that need healing. While most of this book addresses the need for healing in four specific areas, let's begin by examining a story that depicts the overall dynamic of the spiritual recovery process by means of an allegorical reading of the story of the Good Samaritan. As we proceed, please bear with these loose paraphrases of the dialogue of the people in the story.

The Good Samaritan (Luke 10:25–37)

> On one occasion a lawyer stood up to pose him this problem: "Teacher, what must I do to inherit everlasting life?"

The lawyer can represent our conscious ego, well defended, in control with snappy comebacks. He wanted to know the explicit route to righteousness or justification.

> Jesus answered him: "What is written in the law? How do you read it?"

A good "lawyer response" to a lawyer is to ask another question as Jesus did. The lawyer quoted from a book of the law, Deuteronomy:

> He replied: "You shall love the Lord your God with all your heart, with all of your soul, all your strength, and with all your mind, and your neighbor as yourself."
>
> Jesus said, "You have answered correctly. Do this and you shall live."

In this story the lawyer cited an explicit principle out of the book of the law, and if we want an explicit code of life, a left-brain guideline for living, then that is a very good principle. Interpreted allegorically in connection with Jungian psychology, to love God with all your heart (feeling), all of your soul (intuition), all of your mind (thinking), and all of your strength (sensing), includes all four ego functions. It's a complete and thorough devotion of the ego capacity to God. Then, if you love your neighbor as yourself, you are less likely to project onto others damaging or destroying relationships. This is indeed a complete program of life.

> But because he wished to justify himself, he said to Jesus, "And who is my neighbor?"

Our ego is never really satisfied with formulas about the spiritual life and about our growth. Jesus looked at him (looked at the conscious ego in us) and said, in effect, "There's not much comprehension going on in the left side of your brain. I think I'll go in on the right. I'll tell you a story:"

Jesus replied: "There was a man going down from Jerusalem to Jericho . . ."

Jerusalem was a walled city on a hill two thousand feet above sea level, the hub of political and religious activity in Jesus' day. It is a good symbol of our power position, our conscious ego, who we think we are when we're in control of things. Jericho, seventeen miles away, was one thousand feet below sea level near the Dead Sea. To the listener of that time, it was the oldest city known to memory. In fact, it was so ancient, it was earlier than memory. And to the Jewish listener, it evoked an image of the time when the Hebrews crossed the Jordan River into the Promised Land and had to deal with this ancient fortress, Jericho, whose surrounding walls could be shattered only by the power of God. It was "down there," three thousand feet below Jerusalem. Jericho represents the things down in our subconscious minds and back in our pasts that we go after when we make a recovery journey.

So far in this story, we know that a human being left a defended position, left a state of control, and began to journey alone, going down and back.

> . . . who fell prey to robbers. They stripped him, beat him, and then went off leaving him half-dead.

We set out on a program of change, attempting to come to grips with recovery or our conversion or whatever we are grappling with. We think the objective is to get to Jericho and find out all about that old material that drives us, from our family of origin or our alcoholic ancestors, and so forth. And after we move toward this old material for a while, our habits, our compulsions, our circumstances of life, surround us and attack us. Those who have embarked on a diet or tried to give up cigarettes can probably remember what the third day of change is like. It's as if the old habit or desire literally attacks us. It beats us up, bloodies our ego, breaks us and leaves us half-dead by the side of the road. We can't go forward, we can't go backward, and we wonder why we ever tried to make the trip.

The story goes on.

> A priest happened to be going down the same road; he saw him but continued on.

Allegorically, the priest can represent our own conventional attitude toward our brokenness, our need to feel good about ourselves. In those days, touching a corpse rendered a priest unfit for temple duty, so the priest was playing it safe. This attitude of playing it safe represents our ambivalent attitude toward our own brokenness, or whatever is shattered in our lives. At first it is difficult to value whatever has shattered us or even the recovery process.

> Likewise there was a Levite who came the same way; he saw him and went on.

Whereas a priest was appointed to temple duty, a Levite had a privileged position by being born into the tribe of Levi, the priestly tribe. A priest earned the position; a Levite was a temple attendant by birth. The Levite represents another part of us that may feel "entitled," that will not admit or connect to brokenness.

> But a Samaritan who was journeying along came on him and was moved to pity at the sight.

It is difficult to know in our day how Samaritans were regarded by people in those days. It would probably be similar to our opinion of someone like a dope-dealing pornographer. The Samaritans were the people who had been in the northern kingdom but had broken away and had intermarried with worshipers of the fertility cult, those who worshiped Baal. They eventually returned to the God of Abraham and Moses but opposed the Temple cult in Jerusalem and built their own temple on Mount Gezirim. Samaritans were considered loathsome and dangerous, and association with them contaminated one spiritually. That's why in John's Gospel the Samaritan woman was so astonished that Jesus would talk to her (John 4:4–30). A "good Jew" didn't even touch a Samaritan.

Yet in this story, Jesus says that a *Samaritan* comes by. Imagine the most feared and detested side of your personality, the thing that you are most ashamed to admit, the worst thing you know about yourself, comes out of your unconscious, comes over to your ego and *touches* you. This most shameful part of you, a frightening part of your shadow side, is the agent God picks for your salvation, your recovery.

> He approached him and dressed his wounds, pouring in oil and wine.

The Samaritan stopped, took out the first-aid kit of the day, oil and wine, and poured them on the wounds of this bloody and broken fellow. Wine is a penetrating, cleansing astringent, the masculine principle. Oil is a soothing, healing substance that promotes the knitting together of tissue, the feminine principle. At the core of our woundedness, the masculine and feminine unite, and new life is produced.

> He then hoisted him on his own beast . . .

The beast might represent the animal side of us, our raw humanity, not the pretty side of us, but the part of us we think so unworthy that God couldn't possibly love it. We ourselves can barely tolerate it. But it is this side that now carries us.

> . . . and brought him to an inn, where he cared for him.

All through the night (the dark night of the soul), the Samaritan ministers to the one found on the side of the road.

> The next day he took out two silver pieces and gave them to the innkeeper . . .

Could the innkeeper be our new attitude, our appropriate, wiser attitude toward our brokenness?

> . . . with the request: "Look after him, and if there is any further expense I will repay you on my way back."

The Samaritan will be back. The shadow will come back into our lives with its gift. Those who acknowledge that they are sick (broken) are given the opportunity for salvation. Our brokenness, not our strength, is the first instance of us coming together as Christians. We see the face of the same Christ in a "street person" that we see in our own shame and our brokenness. That is evidently where Jesus presents himself.

When people kept being scandalized at how Jesus consorted with outcasts, he said, "It's not the well people who need a physician, it's the sick. I've come for those who need me; I've come for the sick."

Then Jesus turned to the lawyer and asked,

> "Which of these three, in your opinion, was neighbor to the man who fell in with the robbers?"
> And the answer came, "The one who treated him with compassion."
> Jesus said to him, "Then go and do the same."

To the degree we can consciously face the brokenness in ourselves, we are safe to face and touch the brokenness of others, and not before. And so the Samaritan will come back again and again in our lives, bringing a gift of deeper recovery and touching us where we are most afraid.

Incidentally, keeping our sense of humor in all this is important. Teresa of Avila, who was a very busy, good woman, and a very effective reformer in her day, got stuck in the rain on her burro on a Spanish road in a downpour, and the water came up high on the burro's legs. And Teresa looked up at the sky and said, "If this is the way you treat your friends, no wonder you don't have very many!"

The Twelve Steps

Not only our external behavior but also the subconscious part of our being begins to recover when we do something like the Twelve Steps. We will look at how two paths of healing are converging nowadays: psychological healing and the Twelve Steps.

There is a particularly American flavor to the spirituality fostered by the Twelve-Step movement, a spirituality for a pluralistic democratic society that doesn't let dogma get in the way of change or action. This path of coming to wholeness, or recovery, has a lot in common with traditional methods of conversion.

The Twelve Steps of Alcoholics Anonymous have much to offer us in the way of spiritual healing. The authors of these steps didn't get stuck in formal theology, and yet they practiced it by trying to understand real faith in their lives. People in Twelve-Step programs are able to move toward conversion and commitment because they don't get held up by debates about God. Yet there seems to be a strong connection between these steps and traditional Christianity, so that believers can embrace the Twelve-Step form of recovery and benefit from the exciting healing it brings.

The Twelve Steps embody a fourfold healing process that touches on each of the areas of injury we have explored. First, they teach us to connect with a Higher Power as a care giver (Steps One through Three). Second, they lead us into our human reality, helping us to stop blurring it with other people's reality, and readying us to turn to God for healing (Steps Four through Six). Third, the steps guide us as we actually turn to God, who heals us without abusing or enmeshing with us (Step Seven). We continue in our recovery by making restitution in a special way to people for the harm we have done by the way we have misused our power (Steps Eight and Nine). Fourth, the steps develop within us spiritual tools by which we can begin to find the pattern or meaning in our lives (Steps Ten through Twelve).[3]

Moving into a Spiritual Recovery Process

The messages in the Gospels, the parables, and the Twelve Steps suggest various forms of spiritual and psychological healing. Another source of recovery offered in this book is a set of specific psychological exercises to implement these suggestions for healing each area of injury.

The following chapters contain information and exercises for spiritual healing from several sources to apply to each of the four areas of woundedness we have explored: neglect, enmeshment, abuse, and abandonment. The sources include the four Gospels, the parables of Jesus and other stories from the Bible, the Twelve Steps of Alcoholics Anonymous, and specific psychological exercises that have spiritual roots.

NOTES

1. See "History and Interpretation of the Bible," *The Interpreter's Bible,* Vol. 1 (New York: Abingdon Press, 1952), p. 121.
2. We are aware that the parable has historically been thought to be primarily a way to drive home a single point. The present allegorical approach suggests that the richness of meaning extends to the very substratum of the individual human psyche without in any way diminishing the primary point the parable was designed to make.
3. Richard D. Grant, Jr., *Symbols of Recovery: The Twelve Steps at Work in the Unconscious* (Philadelphia: Type and Temperament Press, 1990).

Healing from Neglect

12

The Unmet Need for Perfect Parenting

A problem resulting from experiencing neglect in childhood seems to be that we, as adults, now neglect our own selves, particularly our inner child. This self-neglect stems from the misdirection of our longing for the perfect parent. There seem to be at least two responses to this condition of adult self-neglect: (1) expecting others to parent us, and (2) becoming accustomed to living in a state of self-neglect so that we are unaware that we are self-neglectful.

Expecting Others to Parent Us

Whenever we connect with our own unmet needs, the unsatisfied longing that drives us to continue to seek parenting, we may blame other people in our present circumstances for not parenting us and thereby sabotage our relationships with them. Instead of seeking to be parented by a person, such as a husband or wife, or even by our own parents now that we are adults, we can learn to allow God to give us ultimate parenting. And under God's direction, we can make decisions about parenting those neglected parts of our own inner self. As our need for parenting begins to be met spiritually, our relationships with the people from whom we used to seek parenting can move into a healthier realm because we don't have an unrealistic expectation of what they are "supposed to" be doing for us.

Being Unaware of Our State of Self-Neglect

We may verge on emotional bankruptcy, physical burnout, mental fatigue, or spiritual emptiness, as we move through life sort of numbly making the best of things. We may avoid recognizing our deprivation because such a realization involves pain.

An example of being out of touch and avoiding recognition of adult self-neglect is illustrated by the experience of a woman we name Cindy. After a few years of recovery with traditional counseling and attending Twelve-Step meetings, Cindy undertook nurturing herself. One day she decided to take a walk on a trail by a river in the late afternoon to give herself space to unwind from an especially hectic day. As she walked, she concentrated on breathing deeply, inhaling peace and serenity, and exhaling the tensions and concerns of the day. About twenty minutes into the walk, a wave of painful sadness interrupted her peaceful thoughts, and tears came to her eyes. The pang of sadness continued to the end of the walk. That evening, at a Twelve-Step meeting, she described this experience, and again the tears sprang to her eyes and her voice quavered.

"This is so strange," she said through her tears. "I thought I would feel joy when I was able to nurture myself. Why does it hurt so much?" After several days, she realized that when she did nurture herself she simultaneously had to acknowledge her *need for nurture* with which she had lost touch. This acknowledgment was accompanied by recognition of a seemingly vast chasm of unmet needs within her created by the years of self-neglect. Her pain and sadness came from her new awareness of the reality of living in self-neglect.

For a while her acts of self-nurture continued to be accompanied by pangs of pain and sadness, but with her sense of support and encouragement from God and her Twelve-Step friends she was able to continue to develop her ability to nurture herself in spite of the accompanying pain and sadness. She recognized these feelings as part of her recovery journey, and used them for guidance in choosing self-nurturing behaviors. She began to redirect the deep longing of her precious child for a perfect parent and the natural response of that inner child toward developing a stronger spiritual contact with God, the only Perfect Parent. And her growing trust is that God will not neglect her.

What It Means to Follow Jesus

Some of us have realized that we need to learn to distinguish when we need to take care of ourselves, and when we have the capacity to help others. Yet the idea of refraining from helping others for any reason is strongly resisted by many Christians.

One person asked, "But what if the Good Samaritan had said to the injured man in the ditch, 'I'm sorry you're hurting, but I'm just not able to be there for you today'?" Is always giving to others regardless of our own personal condition what Jesus meant when he asked us to follow him?

Some Christians may think that to follow Jesus means to get up on a cross, sacrificing ourselves for the good of others. But if anything needs to be sacrificed, it is probably our secret messiah complexes, believing we are supposed to be the savior in *any* situation. We seek to follow Jesus Christ, but what does "follow" mean in this context?

Some may think it means to be exactly like Jesus or to copy Jesus. But the problem is that we are *not* exactly like Jesus. We lack what made Jesus a Savior. We are human beings, "made in the image of God," and also, "a little lower than the angels."

One definition of the word *follow* is "to accept as an authority, to obey."[1] Our experience indicates that for healing this is the definition of "following Christ" we need to embrace. We need to allow the words of Jesus and the actions of the Holy Spirit to inform us about how to live—to be filled, restored, nurtured. Then, what we give to others is not ourselves, right down to the last gasp, but the overflowing love, wisdom, and strength we have first received from Christ. If we have not been in some sense filled, restored from our experiences of neglect, and nurtured, we have little or nothing to give.

Unlearning Family-of-Origin Lessons

It's easy to think that as good Christians we should give endlessly to others. Perhaps our parents, our first higher power, taught us either by their own behavior or by demands made on us that we must serve the family—beyond the point of healthy interdependence to the point where our own childhood needs and wants were neglected. Entering adulthood with this ingrained set of values invites trouble in the way we live out our lives and relationships. And even though we have good intentions about being Christians, we may not be following the Way Jesus intended for us to follow.

God implanted within us these deep yearnings for a perfect parent, and God provided the satisfaction for them—connection to God and interdependence with other people. Certain needs can be met only by interaction with another person or people, but if the interaction doesn't have the form, content, and timing that God intended in our inner longings, the need isn't met and the interaction with others may turn out to be destructive to ourselves, to the other person, or both. For example, we may either attempt to control them or fix them, to meet our own needs, and such "giving" is often accompanied by unrealistic expectations about how our giving should be received. We need the knowledge, sensitivity, and attitude of surrender to the power of God moving within and among us through the Holy Spirit to guide us in the decisions and actions of our daily lives. Then we can fulfill that longing to be a loving, responding child to our perfect Parent.

When we drain ourselves for the sake of others, or compulsively set aside the natural course of our lives because of the perceived need of another, we may not be giving what *God* intended us to give at all but rather what *we* think is needed. We may even be interfering with God's best will for that other person, or for ourselves as when a parent continues to try to control a son's or daughter's life—even after he or she is grown.

Sometimes we concentrate so hard on giving that we either do not learn to receive or we forget how to do it. We act as if we must choose between being a giver or a receiver, seeing giving as virtuous and receiving as selfish.

We Must Be a Well, Not a Pipe

Jesus repeated a rule of thumb for serving others: ". . . and you shall love the Lord God with all your heart, and all your soul, and all your strength, and all your mind; and your neighbor as yourself" (Luke 10:27). The commandment does *not* say to love our neighbor *more than* ourselves. Loving our neighbor *as* ourselves focuses our attention on the concept of equal value among all men and women. It implies that we are to operate out of an inner core of self-esteem that tells us we are not less than others, but neither do we put ourselves above anyone. Healthy love of neighbor never excludes healthy love of self.

It follows, then, that we need to learn to give out of resources from within us that come from redirecting our deepest longings to God. Airline cabin attendants instruct adults to put on their own air masks before assisting any children. They know that an unconscious adult with no oxygen will be of little help to a child. In the same way, we must first begin to be healthy ourselves before we can know how God wants us to give to those around us.

NOTE

1. *Webster's New Collegiate Dictionary.*

13

God as a Nurturing Provider: The Gospel of Matthew

The Gospel of Matthew Speaks Directly to Neglect Issues

The Gospel of Matthew addresses the pain of parental neglect. Jesus, talking about the birds and the lilies of the field, tells us in Matthew that our heavenly Parent takes care of us (Matt. 6:26–32). Later, he says, "Seek first the Kingdom of God and its justice and all the rest will be given to you" (Matt. 6:33). In other words, God, the Perfect Parent, knows you need these things and you *will be taken care of.*

There are frequent references to the fulfillment of Old Testament prophecies in Matthew's Gospel. Matthew presents God as being trustworthy; God does not neglect people.

This message strongly suggests that we need to channel that powerful yearning for *perfect* parenting toward God rather than toward other human beings. The focus here is on the parentlike aspect of God—the nurturing Provider who gives us what we need. Shortly after our birth, archetypal energy is released within us so that we can learn to trust and to be open to the care of our parents. As adults in recovery, our goal is to channel the energy from that unsatisfied longing for a perfect parent toward developing trust that what we need will be ultimately provided by God. As this develops, we can stop pressuring and manipulating others to *make* them give us what we need.

Matthew shows us that God cares for us in terms of structure as well as nurture. Matthew's Gospel is full of guidelines, directions, and rules of conduct (see Matt. 5–7, the Sermon on the Mount). There are narratives of how we are to behave when we learn to rely on God for our security. The Gospel of Matthew was used as a handbook for conversion for new Christians in Antioch, and deals with such practical structural issues as church administration and the hierarchy of authority among the apostles.

God combines the feminine (nurture) and masculine (structure) forms of care and cherishes us with characteristics of both a father and mother.

The Temptations of Christ

Jesus had a dramatic experience during the time just after his baptism in which he realized who he was and what he was supposed to do. Looking at this passage allegorically, we can get a clearer picture of how God intends to nurture us and provide us with what we need (Matt. 4:1–11).

Jesus is driven out into the desert by the Spirit, driven out into the wasteland where Israel meets its God, stripped of ordinary self-reliance. The tempter comes to him as he is fasting forty days and says, "If you are the son of God, turn these stones into loaves of bread." It is as if he had said, "Now, Jesus, you can use your special status for material security. You know that. Turn this power into some advantage for yourself. Don't be a fool."

The core issue of this temptation is: do not focus on God as the source of your physical security, as the fail-proof satisfier of this yearning of your heart. You yourself can turn these stones into loaves of bread. The temptation to us today might have a special twist: "With your modern technology, you can literally turn 'stones' into 'loaves of bread', hilltops into shopping centers, seawater into fresh water, atoms into energy. When you have the miracle of technology, do you really need God?"

Jesus replies, "Not by bread alone does man live, but by every word that comes from the mouth of God." He demonstrates the rightful source of physical security—the Word of God.

God Feeds Our Heart's Hunger as Bread Feeds Our Body's Hunger

In John's Gospel Jesus said, "I am the bread of life. Your fathers ate the bread in the desert and died. He who eats this bread will live forever" (John 6:48–51). Jesus is the bread that we are given in the "desert" of our recovery. Jesus is the visible presence of God nurturing us.

We still search for "bread" today, in the slang sense of the word from the 1960s when the term meant money. How do we make our living? What do we really depend on? What do we rely on for our material existence? The "mater" in the word mater-ial is reminiscent of the word *mother*. We often find our emotional security in how we make our living.

Jesus gave us many teachings about how we are to find our security in God, but we hear about this particularly in the Gospel of Matthew. An example is found in Matthew, chapter 6.

> No man can serve two masters. He will either hate one and love the other or be attentive to one and despise the other. You cannot give yourself to God and money.
>
> I warn you then. Do not worry about your livelihood—what you are to eat or drink or use for clothing. Is not life more than food? Is not the body more valuable than clothes?
>
> Look at the birds in the sky. They do not sow or reap; they gather nothing into barns. And yet, your heavenly father feeds them. Are not you more important than they? Which of you, by worrying, can add a moment to his lifespan? As for clothes, why be concerned?
>
> Learn a lesson from the way the wildflowers grow. They do not work, they do not spin, yet I assure you, not even Solomon in all his splendor was arrayed like one of these. If God can clothe in such splendor the grass of the field which blooms today and is thrown on the fire tomorrow, will he not provide much more for you? O weak in faith!
>
> Stop worrying, then, over questions like what are we to eat, what are we to drink, what are we to wear? The unbelievers are always running after these things. Your heavenly father knows all that you need.
>
> Seek first his kingship over you, his way of holiness, and all these things will be given you besides. (Matt. 6:24–33)

In chapter 7 of Matthew, Jesus encourages us to feel and acknowledge our needs as we direct our profound yearning to God in prayer:

> Would one of you hand his son a stone when he asks for a loaf, or a poisonous snake when he asks for a fish? If you, with all your sins, know how to give your children what is good, how much more will your heavenly Father give good things to anyone who asks him! (Matt. 7:9–11)

Caring for Others

In Matthew's Gospel we learn that an earmark of the Christian is to care for needy and dependent people, through providing nurture and structure. As we begin to be healed by being cared for, we can then take care of others, in a healthy way. But we must be open to being cared for and having our own neglect healed, or else we may become *compulsive* and controlling in the way we enter into service of others. To the degree that we confront our own brokenness and need for healing, we are safe to minister unto others.

In Matthew, the term "little ones" is used, which shows a deep concern for whatever needs to be nurtured and protected.

> Make sure you do not scandalize one of these little ones. It would be better for him who scandalizes these little ones to have a millstone tied around his neck and be cast into the sea. (Matt. 18:6)

Matthew presents God as being very concerned about how we treat "little ones"; this is fully developed in Matt. 25:31–46, a summary of the message about neglect found in Matthew. In this passage we can see what is perhaps Jesus' most direct comment about the reversal of the effects of neglect. Jesus tells us that the practical *meeting of people's needs* (the opposite of neglect) is the benchmark of the Christian.

> When the son of man comes in his glory escorted by all the angels of heaven, he will sit upon his royal throne and all the nations will be assembled before him. Then he will separate them into two groups as a shepherd separates sheep from goats.

(Matthew was a tax collector, an accountant of sorts. The sheep and goats are like the final ledgering of debits and credits.)

> The sheep he will place on his right hand. The goats on his left. "Come," the king will say to those on his right. "Come, you have my father's blessing. Inherit the kingdom prepared for you from the creation of the world. For I was hungry and you gave me food. I was thirsty and you gave me drink. I was a stranger and you welcomed me, naked and you clothed me. I was ill and you comforted me, in prison and you came to visit me."
>
> Then the just will ask him, "Lord, when did we see you hungry and feed you or you thirsty and give you drink? When did we welcome you away from home, or clothe you in your nakedness? When did we visit you when you were ill or in prison?"
>
> The king will answer them, "I assure you, as often as you did it for one of these least brothers, you did it for me."
>
> Then he will say to those on his left, "out of my sight, you condemned into that everlasting fire prepared for the devil and his angels! For I was hungry and you gave me no food, I was thirsty and you gave me no drink. I was away from home and you gave me no welcome, naked and you gave me no clothing. I was ill and in prison and you did not come to comfort me."

Then they, in turn will ask: "Lord, when did we see you hungry or thirsty or away from home or naked or ill or in prison and not attend to your needs?"

He will answer them: "I assure you, as often as you *neglected* to do it to one of these least ones, you *neglected* to do it to me." These will go off to eternal punishment and the just to eternal life. [italics ours] (Matt. 25:31–46)

Matthew shows us not only that we are loved and cared for, but that we are to give that love and care to others. But keep in mind, we are to be a well and not a pipe. Our caring for others, like water in a well, is to overflow our brim as we are filled with God's love for us.

Responding to God's Messages in Our Lives

As we saw in chapter 1, Matthew presents Joseph as a model of attentiveness, a very structured, obedient person. Joseph is given visions and messages from God about the care of Mary and the Child, and he *obeys* what the angel says. Joseph is an example of the obedience we are to have when visions and messages from God arise within us in our recovery.

And the Gospel of Matthew effectively offers to us our marching orders from Jesus. Want a trustworthy authority figure? Here he is.

Jesus said, "All authority in heaven and on earth has been given to me. Go, therefore, make disciples of all nations, baptizing them in the name of the Father, and of the Son, and of the Holy Spirit, teaching them to observe all I have commanded you, and lo I am with you always, even unto the consummation of the world." (Matt. 28:18–20)

Our Deepest Need Answered

Matthew's Gospel speaks directly to the pain of having experienced childhood neglect. In Matthew, God is presented as the Perfect Parent, one who nurtures us, provides for us, and cares for us. The Gospel of Matthew points us to the true satisfaction for our heart's yearning for a nurturing parent who knows what we need and provides it and who does not neglect us.

14

Amazing Stories: God's Concern and Attention to Us

Two parables (one from Matthew and one from Luke) have information for us about directing our deep yearning for perfect parenting toward God: the first part of the Sower and the Seed, and the Prodigal Son.

The Sower and the Seed (Matt. 13:3–8)

A sower went out to sow his seed. Some seed fell on the footpath, where it was trampled underfoot and the birds came and gobbled it up.

Some seed fell on rocky soil where it sprang up quickly, but when the sun came up it scorched it and the plant withered, because it had no depth of root.

Some seed fell among thorns and the plant sprang up, but the thorns sprang up with it and the thorns choked the plant.

And, finally, some seed feel on fertile ground—on good soil. It went in deep and then it sprang up and yielded an abundant harvest, 30, 60 and 100 fold.

Just imagine how they sowed seed in Jesus' time. Without our modern techniques of planting, they had to throw many kernels into a field with little control over where the seed fell.

In the parable of the sower and the seed, Jesus mentioned four soil conditions: the footpath, rocky soil, among thorns, and fertile ground. Our childhood injuries can be represented by the four soil conditions, and the seed symbolizes the Word of God, life itself.

The footpath represents the childhood injury of neglect. The beaten path is the dirt that has been so pressed down (oppressed) by everybody else getting their needs met that the seed can't even get in.

Jesus, being such an astute observer of people, saw that some of us don't seem to "wake up" to life. We just drift on through life and then disappear. For example, one of the adult symptoms that results from being neglected is not being able to represent our needs very well. At work, for example, we might feel it is too difficult to ask for a raise, or we expect the company to take care of us without our having to ask. We may go in and out of depression without knowing it, and seem never to have flowered; we are beaten down (and oppressed) before we've really begun to live.

The birds of the air that come and gobble up the seed symbolize all the distracting, competing forces in life that keep us from our inner spiritual journey. They get their needs met and cut us off from our deepest needs.

We have distraction galore in our culture. Cable TV can keep us distracted from womb to tomb. The media generally conditions us to be vigilant and fearful about what bad thing could happen next. Advertising attempts to create needs within us, distracting us with promises of happiness if only we would buy a certain product. And sometimes we are simply "gobbled up"—eaten up with worry about our security.

And so the seed, the Word of God about how to live, never gets in, and we never realize what a full life is. We are swallowed by other forces in our lives before a seed of new life can germinate in us. Without spiritual recovery, we may remain essentially unconscious of our spiritual and personal potential. This unawareness is a core adult symptom of childhood neglect.

Jesus spoke directly to such people, saying to those in his day, "Wake up! You have got to watch, to remain aware of these things!" With utter realism, Jesus saw that such people hardly ever became conscious of their authentic needs. They were so beaten down by the weight of tradition that their denial was almost impenetrable.

The Prodigal Son (Luke 15:11–32)

We treat ourselves to a great extent the way we were treated in childhood. If we were neglected as children, we tend to neglect ourselves in adulthood. The part of us that most often gets neglected is the inner vulnerable part, the personification of our early thinking, feeling, and behavior. It is often called the precious child within.

What does God tell us about how to regard our inner child when as adults we finally come into contact with this part of ourselves? On the surface, it would seem that most of us would have a fairly positive attitude toward our inner child, yet many of us take stances ranging from uncertainty and anxiety to being scared to death. In fact, by examining our attitude toward children in general, and how we feel about spending time with children, we can get some insight into how we may feel about our own inner child.

Let's reexamine, in modern dress, a splendid story that allegorically describes our own experience especially at midlife, when we contact our inner child, this part of ourselves that has been neglected. It goes like this.

There was a man who had two sons. The younger son said to his father, "Dad, give me my half of the inheritance in cash. I want to go for it." We'll call this younger son the Kid.

The father said "Sure." He loved his son, and gave him the money. And so the Kid went overseas and spent the money on beautiful women, fine wine, and offshore oil drilling.

He was going to try to make a lot of money. He went for the "window" of investment. Kids are like that; they have a sense of play and risk. Well, he ran out of money, and he couldn't phone home or send a message by Western Union, so he went to work on a pig farm in this foreign country. Then a famine struck the land. And there he was, sitting in the pigpen, and his employers wouldn't even give him the husks that they were feeding the swine.

And so the Kid, being ever resourceful, said, "This is bad! How many of my father's hired hands have more than enough to eat while here I sit in a foreign country starving to death? I know what I will do. I will go back to my father and I'll say, 'Father, I have sinned against heaven and against you. I don't deserve to be called your son. Make me a hired hand.' At least I will eat." So, off he goes.

While the Kid is a long way off, the father sees him coming and runs out to meet him. And the boy says, "Father, I have sinned against heaven and against you. I don't deserve to be called your son. Make me a hired hand."

And the father embraces him and kisses him on the neck and says, "Quick, get him a new shirt, a fresh pair of jeans and some new boots. Let's kill the fatted calf and have a barbecue. For my son was dead, and now he is alive. He was lost, and he has been found."

And the Kid says, "A party! All right!" Notice how the father understood the boy, and how he spoke the boy's language—celebrating the moment of the boy's return.

Meanwhile, the older brother was out in the field, the older brother part of us. This older brother plowed those fields, dawn to dusk. As many of us who are firstborn, he was very responsible! He had just about plowed under the land that the Kid left fallow when the Kid went overseas to blow half the family fortune on wild women and wine. He angrily thought of the Kid as he muscled his way through some particularly tough clods of dirt.

He came in from plowing at 7:00 P.M., and as he came home, hot and sweaty, he heard music coming from the family farm. Now, he didn't mind parties that were on the family budget, but this party wasn't budgeted.

And he asked a servant, "What is going on?"

And the servant said, "Oh, your younger brother, the one that went overseas? Well, he has come home, and your father killed the fatted calf for *him*."

The older brother is stunned. "Whatever happened to 'work hard and then you will get your reward'?!!" he wonders. "He was bad and he's getting a reward. I was good and I'm getting ignored! I mean, I don't understand—it's wrong!" the brother rants. This may be something like how it feels "when bad things happen to good people," like getting an illness that won't go away, or having marriage trouble, or seeing that the kids aren't turning out right, or finding out our job is going nowhere. We thought we had an agreement with God, who would protect us if we were good. Almost all of us can probably identify with this aspect of ourselves.

The older, responsible brother gets very angry when things get out of control, because he bases his self-esteem on staying in control. He then *angrily* sends in for his father.

The father comes out to the older boy, just as he came out to the younger one. And the older boy says, "Father, how long have I slaved for you, all these years, not even asking for a goat to have with my friends. I am frugal, you know. But when your younger son comes home, who, let me remind you, has wasted half the family fortune on wild women and wine, you kill the fatted calf for him. It is *not* fair!"

And the father turned to his son and he said, "My son [or he could say, my daughter], you are with me always, and everything I have is yours. It is a gift. You don't earn it. And so, we must rejoice when your brother comes home. Because he was dead, and now he is alive. He was lost and he has been found." And then the father turned and went into the party (I always like to think, adding under his breath, "and you need him, son, if you get my meaning"), leaving the older brother standing there.

Often, at midlife our "Kid," our inner child, comes home. In early life, in the name of education and doing the right thing and earning a living, many of us stomp the Kid out of our conscious repertoire and into the muck and mire of the instinctual unconscious—the pigpen in a foreign country. We have usually repressed that "Kid" side of us. But frequently, at midlife, the Kid comes back home, that is, back to our conscious personality. All those things that we are afraid of, instinctive, animalistic, bodily, the "other" sides of us, back they come with the Kid at midlife. And God, our perfect Parent, rejoices at this encounter and throws a party for this Kid!

This story gives us a model for our attitude toward our inner child. God loves our Kid, and if we have a hard time loving our Kid, maybe we can begin to soften, and come to believe in the Kid the way God, our perfect Parent, believes in the Kid and welcomes this precious child home.

But back to the story and the older brother. One way we might envision this story ending is this:

> The older brother just can't endure going in to the party. And so he goes up to his bedroom, takes a shower, and then sits on the edge of his bed for several hours reading *Farming Today*. He is waiting for the music to die down, when he can go down and help clean up, so that nothing will be wasted.
>
> At about two in the morning, the music dies down and he goes out to the head of the stairs to go down and help clean up. Who should be at the bottom of the stairs but the Kid, who joyfully says "Brother!" and runs up the stairs and embraces the older boy. The older brother stiffens while the Kid says, "You are the one I wanted to see! I went overseas and I was going to take our money and invest in an offshore oil rig. Big investment window there! I had to go for it, you know. By the way, they had the most beautiful women over there, and fine wine, too! You ought to go someday. But hey, I lost the money. I am sorry. But you know what? There was a famine there and I got a job in a pigpen. Can you imagine me in a pigpen?"
>
> And the Kid rushes on, "I watched how they raised livestock over there. They do it differently."
>
> Now the older boy gets interested. The Kid starts describing livestock production techniques in the foreign country. And the older brother gets very interested in this and then puts these ideas into operation, and the next year they triple livestock production.
>
> So they put the older brother in charge of operations and the Kid in charge of marketing and PR and they have a great farm from then on!
>
> And the father loves them *both*.

God loves both of these sides of us. An important part of channeling our need for nurture to God is that we begin to appreciate and love the Kid in us. In addition, as our yearning for homecoming is satisfied by our heavenly Parent, we can turn and care for others, and get on with our lives as persons who are more whole. Receiving God's love and care is the authentic source of our ability to care for others.

15

Redirecting Our Deep Longing for Perfect Parenting to God

Several avenues guide us toward redirecting our deep longing for perfect parenting toward God. In this chapter, we will cover a portion of the Twelve Steps of Alcoholics Anonymous, some journaling about the lessons found in the parables, and some psychospiritual exercises.

The Twelve Steps: Steps One, Two, and Three[1]

When we enter recovery through the Twelve Steps of Alcoholics Anonymous (whether we apply them to alcoholism, codependence, sin, or any compulsion),[2] we find that the first three steps address our yearning for perfect nurturing and security. The First Step says, "We admitted we were powerless over whatever it is we are trying to get to take care of us (or to numb the pain of being "uncared for"), whatever we are compulsive about, and that our lives have become unmanageable."

We've neglected ourselves, and we've inflicted our self-neglect on others. We can't manage. We can begin to see how this unmanageability ties in to our neglect. We've given up on the inner child, who is running rampant.

Unmanageability stems from the consequences we have of trying to force other people, substances, or experiences to nurture us the way we need to be nurtured. When we channel that deep desire to be cared for toward anything other than God, we suffer the consequences—our lives are incomplete, unsatisfying, frustrating, pain-filled—unmanageable.

The Second Step says, "We came to believe that a Power greater than ourselves could restore us to sanity." This step asks us to consider that there is an alternative approach to life that does not rely on our own power to make others care for us. It suggests that there is a power greater than ourselves that can take care of us and restore us. This step directs us toward that Higher Power as our care giver. This wonderful term describes God theologically to a T. God certainly has powers greater than anything or anyone else. God is the only power we can count on never to fail.

The Third Step says, "We made a decision to turn our will and our lives over to the care of God as we understood God." This step starts with our making a decision. All forms of change seem to begin with a decision, whether we are conscious of the moment of decision or not. The same is true when we change the focus of our deep archetypal yearning for perfect parenting, for the care giving we missed as children, away from ultimate dependence on other people or things and toward God. This step directly refers to an experience of God taking care of us.

These first three steps teach us how to link up with the Higher Power who is the Perfect Parent and does not neglect us. And although God (as a theological figure) is not named in the Twelve Steps, in the first three steps we experience what Christians call God the Parent, an all-encompassing blend of fatherlike and motherlike qualities.

People in recovery using the Twelve-Step process often say, "You can't give what you haven't got," meaning "don't try to help someone recover by way of the Twelve Steps until you've done the steps yourself and have been changed by them." The steps begin at the first level of development, that of developing trust and being open to the experience of being cared *for* by the Perfect Parent for whom our hearts have longed all the while. The steps change us by teaching the humility and dependence on God that is necessary for recovery and for helping others. They first teach us to receive: from others who have something to give, from the Higher Power who restores us to sanity if we are faithful to follow, and from the Twelve-Step process as an authoritative path for recovery.

The Lessons in the Parables

Review the stories in chapter 14 and apply them to your own life by responding to the questions below. Write your responses in your journal.

The Sower and the Seed

1. What distractions in your life today keep you from feeling a need for spiritual contact with God?

2. How do you earn your "bread"? (On what do you rely for material security?)
3. What feelings (emotions) and attitudes (thoughts or opinions) do you have about your inner child? Write about feelings separately from thoughts and opinions.
4. As an adult, from what other people have you tried to get the parenting you missed as a child? With what result?

Psychospiritual Exercises

The issue of neglect is hard to face in therapy because it's related to things that *didn't* happen to us, and so it is particularly *unconscious*. We who were neglected children can as adults deny what happened (or didn't happen) to us and develop a myth about how wonderful childhood was and how great our parents were, because of our deep yearning for the perfect parent. When we finally do face neglect issues, we may experience much pain and loss as we give up these myths about our childhood and our parents.

To recover, it's important to realize that although our interaction with our parents activated a deep, but unsatisfied, yearning in us, we can now get that yearning fulfilled in other ways.

Both of the following exercises relate to reversing neglect as we recognize God's coming to us through the love of other people who affirmed us for simply being here as a precious child, and through the delight we experienced in certain events.

These exercises are something of a counterbalance to our painful childhood memories. Sometimes when we are in therapy, we think that all we can remember are painful experiences. If we're not careful, we may wind up needing more therapy to "get over" therapy, because the immersion in painful memories may convince us that our lives are nothing but tragedies. We may get so accustomed to dealing with the pain that we rarely deal with our positive memories.

But it's just as important to remember the delightful, enjoyable experiences of our lives, because they become the foundation of developing an awareness that our lives weren't as deeply tragic as we might think, but rather filled with both goodness and joy as well as pain and injury. Yes, we do need to search diligently for memories of events that hurt us; we need to deal with them and work toward an attitude of forgiveness. But both of the following exercises are a counterbalance to a tendency to make our painful memories the focal point of our lives.

Life Affirmation Baseline

This positive, gentle exercise will help acquaint you with how God has cared for you over your lifetime. The Life Affirmation Baseline guides you to recall people who accepted you just for who you are. These can be friend, teacher, parent, and so on, across your lifetime.

Although we may not have much nurturing to imitate in our family of origin, we can empower ourselves by looking at any relationships that created the correct conditions for our being affirmed. *We can learn to imitate these people's behavior toward us in our care for our own inner child.*

Some people wonder, "How do I nurture my own children if I wasn't nurtured? I feel so empty, and I don't have anything inside me from which to draw in order to take care of them. I just feel so limited. I'm not very nurturing. How do you give what you didn't get?"

In addition to the slow process of recovery through counseling, there is additional good news for a Christian. We're not on our own in being saved from the effects of childhood neglect. God cares for us and will provide us information about how we can nurture ourselves. The following exercise provides one of the ways we can access this information.

What to Do

1. Draw several rows of three circles, each large enough to contain a single word.

2. In each of the circles, write the name of one of the people you feel has simply accepted you. By acceptance, we mean that you did not have to be intelligent, good-looking, or hardworking for these people. You could relax around them. They communicated to you that they liked you simply for being you. These people could have been known to you in childhood or in adulthood: childhood friends, current friends, family members, work associates, Twelve-Step sponsors, and so forth. The relationships may have ended, but if they existed for enough time to be important to you, place the person's name in one of the circles.

Note: It is not necessary to fill in every circle, but if you do, and still have other names in mind, just draw more circles for them. If it is hard to think of names easily right now, try not to be discouraged. Just start the mental search process, keep it in mind, and add names as they come to you over the next few days or weeks.

The important thing for this exercise is not so much *who* these people were, although that is important, but *what they did* that made you feel accepted.

3. Below the circles write what each person did that made you feel cherished, cared about, special, accepted.

The people whose names you've written in the circles are like sacraments; they are your teachers about God's care for you. Many of us don't know what being nurtured feels like. To feel with your heart's radar that someone accepts you is to feel what it's like to be nurtured.

Examples

SALLY: Saved a seat on the school bus for me each morning.

MR. NORWOOD: Coach who told me he liked my spunk after I had been tack-led especially hard in a practice game.

AUNT ROSE: Sat with me and knitted while I did my homework.

WITHERS: Janitor at work who remembered my name the day after we introduced ourselves to each other.

HANK: Brought me flowers for no reason.

JANIE: A co-worker who invited me to a party when I had just moved to town and didn't know anyone.

4. The personification of our emotional life is often called our "inner child of the past." When asked, many people can actually say how old this emotional being is inside themselves. This child accompanies us throughout our days. We as adults have to become the nurturing parent for that inner child that perhaps the child didn't have years ago. We have to be as attentive to raising this inner child as we would to any child outside our skin. We need to be patient with this child. The child is the embodiment of our spontaneous emotional reactions. By reviewing the actions of affirming persons toward us, we can find ways to im-itate what these people did for us as they connected to and affirmed our inner child.

We can learn to love, nurture, and care for ourselves because we can now see how God our Parent has come to us through these people.

Write about experiences you have had as you begin to apply what you have learned in this exercise to your own nurture of yourself.

Examples

I chose a special seat in a restaurant for myself—on the patio near a flowering plant—when I stopped off for lunch yesterday. This is a conscious way to nurture myself because I usually try to take an inconspicuous seat so I wouldn't take up a good seat someone else might like.

I slipped on the ice in the parking lot, and instead of blushing, or getting angry, I laughed! I remembered my "spunk" that Mr. Norwood admired, and got right back up and went on my way.

I brought the checkbook into the den where my wife was reading by the fire and paid the bills while enjoying a companionable silence with her. I enjoyed not having to do that chore alone. It reminded me of having Aunt Rose's clicking knitting needles near me while doing homework.

I took a small ivy plant from the kitchen to work and set it on the windowsill. It was nice to have a living green plant to brighten up my office.

I invited myself to join an exercise class at the YWCA (or YMCA), even though I didn't know anybody. I need the exercise and yet had avoided it, hoping to meet someone already in a class who would invite me to go with him or her.

Success Experience Baseline[3]

This exercise deals with neglect by looking at *events* that have been affirming (as contrasted with the *people* who have been affirming identified in the first exercise). This process brings us to greater awareness of times when our deepest longings were being met by God, even if we were unaware of it.

When we've had a day that's delightful or enjoyable, we often don't associate that experience with God's touching us at the point of one of our deep longings. This exercise aims at discovering the action of God behind the common elements of these experiences. To develop skill in loving ourselves, it's helpful to find out what makes us feel delighted. We can then begin to build the elements of these experiences into our adult lives to better care for our inner child. Building these into our work environment or adding them to our family environment will help us connect to the satisfactions provided for us by God the Perfect Parent. We can use our memories of our past satisfying experiences to construct a life plan for recovery.

Because unconsciousness accompanies neglect, many of the elements that make up a good day for us may lie just below our threshold of awareness. We never really tease out just what it is that makes us feel good. The following exercise helps us increase our awareness of these positive elements.

This exercise also illustrates the grace of God touching us when we're feeling the delight and joy called *serendipity*.

What to Do

You will need at least an hour and a half for this exercise. It is divided into three parts. You can do each part in a separate sitting, or work through all three parts at once.

1. Review your life for specific experiences that you have found satisfying. Include experiences from any part of your life, such as a job, a friendship, a trip, working, playing on a team, a hobby, and so on. The only important criterion for these experiences is that *you* enjoyed them, no matter what anyone else felt.

It helps to divide your life into three-year segments, using your right-brain picture memory to locate the approximate date, setting, and companions. For example, in remembering a satisfying experience between ages seven and nine, you might start by *picturing* your house, neighborhood, backyard, church, school building, or any other *place* that was in your life at the time. Thinking about these settings can trigger memories of satisfying or delightful experiences that happened to you. It is surprising how accurate the details can be, because we tend to remember vividly those experiences we enjoy.

Label each experience you remember with a phrase, then write down the phrases next to the three-year segment in which the experience occurred. Continue remembering, labeling, and writing down experiences until you come to your present age.

Note: You may be able to complete this exercise quickly and accurately, but if nothing comes for a while, don't worry. Just write down your impressions as they come to you over the next few days and weeks.

Examples

Ages	Experience
0–3	Running at the beach
4–6	Fifth year birthday party
	Building fort with Steve
7–9	Making my own Halloween costume
	Singing in a Christmas concert with my class
10–12	Camping overnight with scout troop
	Collecting money on my paper route

2. Next, write the phrase that labels your first remembered experience at the top of a sheet of paper. Recall in vivid, concrete detail the surroundings of your

experience. Don't leave out any impression you remember. Write details in the four categories described next:

1. *Physical Environment:* Where were you? Inside/outside; day/night; hot/cold; alone/crowded; technical/natural; loud/quiet, and so forth.
2. *Social Environment:* What kind of people were you with? Young/old; enthusiastic/calm; loud/quiet; aesthetically attractive/didn't matter, and so forth. Each of us has preferences for companionship; it's not snobbish to have social preferences.
3. *Activity:* What were you doing? Talking/listening, agreeing/persuading, manual manipulation/nonmanual work such as seeing, thinking, appreciating, and so on.
4. *Reward:* What was it about the experience that was most enjoyable or satisfying for you? Seeing your work finished, friendship, aesthetic delight, recognition from a respected authority, money, recognition from peers, altruistic satisfaction, and so on.

Write these four paragraphs for each experience on a single page, using a separate page for each experience. Before you leave this part of the exercise, you will have a number of experiences (one per sheet), fully detailed as described. Use a sheet for each experience you listed in step 1. Complete this part for each experience before moving to step 3.

Example

Running at the beach

(Copy the phrase you used in step 1 to identify one of the experiences on the top of a sheet of paper)

Physical Environment: Outdoors, summer, morning, sound of sea gulls, uncrowded.

Social Environment: With my older cousins Amy and Bitsy.

Activity: Running, shouting, laughing, Amy was chasing me, hugging me, Bitsy was holding my hand.

Reward: Physical activity, enjoyed Amy's and Bitsy's attention, sense of freedom.

3. Place the sheets of paper side by side on a large table so that all the titles line up together. Comb through the experiences *across* each of the four sections. For example, read the "Physical Environment" sections of all the experiences you have described. Look for any patterns or consistencies in them.

These consistencies across experiences help define who you are when you are at your best. They are the time-tested elements that truly nurture you. Building these into your life and responding to their positive effects is a way to make a conscious connection to the God who nurtures us.

Write any patterns you discover on a summary sheet, using the format shown here:

Consistencies

Physical Environment:
Social Environment:
Activity:
Reward:

NOTES

1. See Appendix A for all twelve Steps as they were developed by Alcoholics Anonymous.
2. See Keith Miller, *A Hunger for Healing: The Twelve Steps as a Classic Model for Spiritual Growth* (San Francisco: Harper San Francisco, 1991) for Christians who do not have a recognizable addiction and would like background and a specific discussion about how to use the Twelve Steps for spiritual growth.
3. This exercise is similar to the work of Richard N. Bolles, *What Color Is Your Parachute?* (Berkeley, CA: Ten Speed Press, 1992), but is considerably shorter.

Healing from Enmeshment

16

The Unmet Need for Perfect Companionship and Emotional Development

Experiencing childhood enmeshment leads to our having unrealistic attitudes and expectations about how to relate to others in adulthood. The unrealistic attitudes and expectations we have in our relationships may vary. One form they may take is that without healthy boundaries we may experience pain in our relationships with certain people when differences between us and them become evident. To alleviate the pain, we often capitulate to the will and opinion of the other people.

For example, Harry was a classical music buff and high school tennis champion. When he arrived at college, he discovered that many of the other boys enjoyed playing chess or bridge, two subjects he knew little about. The more Harry learned about his potential friends and the differences between himself and them, the more his shame and doubt grew. To relieve this emotional pain, Harry spent time learning chess, although he regularly lost matches. He neglected going to concerts or playing tennis in favor of pursuing the interests of his new friends. At spring break, he went with these boys to a luxury hotel and spent far beyond his means while hiding his financial anxiety.

Another variation of unrealistic attitudes or expectations is that we may have the sense of being invaded or overrun by others. As a result, we may either avoid relationships or be extremely controlling because normal give and take contact with others is too painful to tolerate.

For instance, Bill avoids shopping for items the family needs with his wife because he fears his preferences will be overrun by her need or desire for him to do everything her way.

Whichever route we take, we tend to enter adulthood without a clear sense of being distinct individuals. The line between ourselves and others is blurred and indistinct; it feels unsafe to relax and be truly ourselves.

Projection

Another factor that further complicates matters is that we seem to be more likely to color or slant our perception of others with *projection*—automatically attributing to other people or events aspects of ourselves of which we are not aware, usually our shadow side or a difficult growth area. Although the other people or events *may not have these characteristics,* we believe they do.

OPPOSITE-SEX PROJECTION

The deepest level of our psyche is often signaled to us by projections that occur on people of the opposite sex. These vital signals may be projections of either our shadow side or of a positive attraction.

Opposite-sex projections of our shadow side are often the deepest and the most devastating, and the hardest to own, because we think that the irritating aspect is a typical trait of the other gender—not something we ourselves could exhibit. How often we say, "Isn't that just like a man," or "just like a woman." Yet the point of reference of the opposite sex within us is called in Jungian terms our "Soul's Companion" and is the gateway into our unconscious. If we don't get in touch with these shadow-side characteristics within ourselves, we close a valuable avenue to our own growth. The more we come to grips with how these traits operate in us, the less likely we will be irritated by this same trait in the other person.

For example, Joe's wife came home from shopping for clothes, arms loaded with packages. Joe's first reaction is anger. His ability to appreciate her enjoyment and accomplishment is overshadowed by his need to ask, "And how much did *that* cost?" Joe can use his anger as a signal warning him to examine his own thinking and feelings about spending money on clothes for himself. He can begin to acknowledge that he is worth spending time, attention, and money on, and then start exploring his tastes and preferences regarding clothes. Any serious problems created by his wife's spending, such as overspending the family's income, can be dealt with in a less "emotion-laden" atmosphere, and Joe would be much less likely to be irritated by seeing his wife's shopping bags on her return from buying clothes.

It is important to examine some aspects of the opposite-sex part of us deep within our unconscious because today so much is promised to people in the name of sexual relationships. We tend to expect overall personal fulfillment and completion in our erotic relationships; some of us even call our sexual partner our "other half." But the "other half" that we are drawn toward is also the "other half" of *ourselves* (all of our unconscious potential). This is the contact point for connecting with God, our Great Lover, who gives us the gift of ourselves. We are projecting *our* positive potentials onto the sexually beloved.

Sexual energy is directed toward greater life. We are usually attracted to characteristics in others that we need to develop within ourselves, in order to have "more abundant life." For example, an attraction leading to sexual intercourse can produce a child (more life) or a deep intimacy (also more life). Often, some of the attractiveness of our beloved involves projected potentials of our own of which we are not yet aware. We "see" these qualities in our beloved, and seek to "unite" ourselves with them by uniting with our beloved.

For instance, early one Saturday morning Dr. Grant took his three sons to a local barber college for inexpensive haircuts. He said:

> As we were sitting there all lined up, the barber student arrived. I guessed her to be about eighteen years old. She was tan and athletic, carried a jam box, wore leather cuffs, and her hair was done in a punk wave. My heart went "B-o-i-n-g."
>
> I said to myself, "Oh no. Give me a break. I don't need this!" And then, I remembered that she might be an image of my unconscious needs speaking to me. I conjured up her image in my mind and asked, "Well, who are you?"
>
> And in my inner mental picture she replied, "I'm Fun. Let's go play volleyball down at the beach."
>
> I began to realize that my attraction was to the *qualities* I saw in her *image:* youthfulness, health, playfulness, enjoyment of being outdoors, carefree. And this was a most timely message from my unconscious, because I'd been working nights, after my regular hours, on a paper for a conference that was going to "change thinking in the West as we know it!" Needless to say, I was getting much too serious about it, and it was affecting my health. And then this technicolor reaction was given to me. By having a brief dialogue with this image in my mind, I got the message from my unconscious. The message from this opposite-sex projection was, "Get out of doors, lighten up, calm down, enjoy life because you're hurting your health." I realized I needed to get in touch with these qualities in my own life. The erotic image was exactly what I needed to get "in touch" with—inside myself!

The basic rule might be: *we should pay close attention to what we find sexually fascinating in others, because that may be the "road map" of where we will grow next.*

A Double Burden of Distorted Perceptions

After the yearning for perfect companionship has been activated in our family upbringing, we enter adulthood with the belief that somewhere there is a perfect companion, someone with whom we can always be comfortable. When our inborn longing for perfect companionship becomes misdirected, we may follow a disappointing path. First, we may engage in an exhaustive search for the perfect companion for our life's journey, experiencing chronic disappointment with those who do not live up to our ideal expectations. Second, we may be locked in a belief (by the process of projection) that others have weaknesses, disagreeable aspects, or attractive qualities when actually they are aspects of ourselves. When we project these things, we can't see who others really are and we can't form healthy relationships with them.

Instead of looking for the perfect companion (spouse, friend) and being disappointed or shattered when various candidates "let us down" (they exhibit an imperfection or fail to live up to an attribute we thought we saw in them), we can learn to withdraw such idealized expectations from our day-to-day relationships. We do this first by directing this longing to a person who cannot fail our deepest expectations. For a Christian, this involves developing a relationship with Jesus Christ, who is the perfect Companion. He will respect our personal boundaries and affirm us as unique persons.

The result is that our ability to develop interpersonal relationships with *people* improves dramatically, because we don't have such unrealistic expectations that they can give us *everything* that we need emotionally. Our relationship to Jesus Christ will soothe the deep pain of unmet childhood needs (see Matt. 19:13–15), leaving us with a clearer sense of how to work out satisfying relationships in our day-to-day lives.

In Jesus Christ we have a constant source of nonabusive fulfillment for this companionship need. And in recovery we can learn to develop boundaries, so that others don't overrun our space. As people move in and out of our lives, we can stand both the discomfort of starting over with new people and the grief of parting, because of the underlying constancy of a relationship with Jesus Christ. And as the people in long-term relationships with us grow and change (e.g., parents, spouse, children), we can more easily tolerate letting them go into the life choices God has for them, without that heartrending fear that the changes they make will be harmful for them, or will disappoint us, or take them away from us.

RECOVERING CONNECTIONS

17

God as a Companion for Life's Journey:
The Gospel of Luke

The Gospel of Luke speaks to the problem of those who have experienced childhood enmeshment. Luke was known as "beloved physician" and was very interested in healing and wholeness.

Just as the Gospel of Matthew was like a "how-to" handbook for conversion, the Gospel of Luke is like a novel about relating. Luke writes about personalities in relationships and draws them in vivid detail. We are attracted to this gospel because the characters develop as real individuals.

Luke uses a journey theme to represent life. Jesus is presented not so much as the new Moses, or the Rabbi, as he is in Matthew, but as the Companion along the way. He is portrayed as kind of a traveling teacher (which was a literary image often used in classical days), who walks along with people and dialogues with them, but doesn't overwhelm them. Luke paints the picture of Christ as one who will be with us on the way and who will never violate our boundaries, even in the name of healing or teaching.

For example, the first chapter of Luke recounts a most delicate sexual matter between the angel of God, Gabriel, and Mary, a young woman in Nazareth. The angel of God interacted with Mary about this most delicate sexual choice. The whole encounter was transacted with emotional realism and yet freedom of choice. Mary was not violated. Profound respect was shown for her freedom and sensitivity. It's a wonderful example of interacting without enmeshment. The honor given to Mary as Virgin as well as Mother throughout the centuries seems to underscore God's respect for boundaries, for the wholeness and spiritual integrity of this young woman.

Luke's writing balances masculine and feminine. He has as many heroines in the stories as heroes. Males do not enmesh females; they do not consider them mere extensions of masculine need. Luke is sensitive to the poor, to the underprivileged. He appears to recognize that we *all* have poor and underprivileged aspects, not just the people onto whom we project these traits. In presenting Jesus Christ, Luke addresses our heart's yearning for a perfect love relationship—for someone who is lovable, approachable, who doesn't overwhelm us. But Luke also attacks projection and cuts to the heart of enmeshment.

Jesus' Words: Dealing with Our Adversary (Matt. 5:25–26)

Although found in Matthew rather than Luke, this teaching regarding our projected shadow needs to be mentioned here. Jesus said, "Come to terms with your adversary, while you are still on the way, for I am telling you, when you get to the judge, the judge may hand you over to the bailiff, and the bailiff over to the jailer and you will be put in jail, and you won't get out until you have paid the last penny" (Matt. 5:25–26).

Jesus is referring to a Jewish custom that was practiced during his time. Parties involved in lawsuits walked together to court. The idea was to give them an opportunity to settle their dispute on the way to court, because they couldn't be sure of what was going to happen when they came before the judge.

Think of this in terms of dealing with your shadow side. The message is, Come to terms with your shadow, your inner adversary, who may have a case against you—the denied aspects of yourself—while you are yet on the way—while you are still conscious of projecting. Because you have to deal with this part of you, or you risk being imprisoned in a "jail" of unconscious compulsion and addiction, acting out those denied aspects of your personality. And you won't lose the compulsion until you have acknowledged and worked through these denied aspects ("paid the last penny" psychologically).

Jesus Restoring Boundaries Without Enmeshing: The Road to Emmaus (Luke 24:13–35)

The story of the two disciples who journeyed to Emmaus is a good example of a particularly Lucan story that illustrates what it is like to develop good boundaries.

First, the framework of a physical journey symbolizes life. Luke has many accounts of Jesus journeying with his disciples. In this story, he is again journeying with them on the way to Emmaus. The two travelers seem to be feeding upon each other's misery and confusion.

Then Jesus comes and stands between them, and says, in essence, "What are you talking about?"

They say, "Haven't you heard? Are you the only one who didn't know about it?" And they talk about all the bad things that happened in Jerusalem to Jesus, the one they thought was going to lead them as the Messiah. Then Jesus clarifies an interpretation of Scripture, saying, "Oh, what little sense you have! Don't you understand, he had to go through all this in order to enter into his glory?" The story goes on to say, "And then he opened up their minds to all of the meaning of the Scriptures that pertained to him."

When they got to the end of the journey, Jesus seems to be about to leave them and the disciples say, "Stay with us." Jesus agrees to eat with them. When he breaks the bread, they recognize him. Later they say, "Were not our hearts burning within us while he was with us on the way?"

After Jesus breaks the bread, he disappears. The verb Luke used for "disappears" has the connotation of "becomes invisible, but is still present." The outward appearance of Jesus disappeared along with the disciples' projected hope for a political messiah. By this we mean that the renewal of their beliefs about Jesus' real mission involved their first developing healthy intellectual and spiritual boundaries. Using these new healthy boundaries, they could then see *Jesus'* reality about his mission as separate from *their own* reality based on hope for a political messiah.

He answered not only the questions in their minds about the meaning of the Scriptures, but also the yearning of their hearts for perfect companionship. Such personal integration of mind and heart is the result of a healthy relationship, one that heals and affirms without violating.

Today, Jesus is still present, but invisible. God continues to heal our human projection that enmeshes God, that wants God on our terms.

Our Deepest Need Answered

Luke's Gospel answers our deepest needs for intimacy and emotional growth, presenting an appropriate, unfailing Object for our yearnings for a perfect companion. Luke's Gospel directly addresses the pain of having experienced childhood enmeshment. God is presented by Luke as coming to meet us in the person of Jesus Christ, the perfect Companion for life's journey, the one who travels with us, teaching us and restoring our boundaries. Luke's Gospel offers the true satisfaction for our heart's yearning for a relationship with someone who respects our boundaries, yet provides a guiding presence throughout our lives.

18

Amazing Stories: God's Companionship in Our Lives

There are numerous stories and parables that give us a model for redirecting toward God our deep yearning for a perfect companion. We will begin with two parables and two stories from Luke's Gospel, then also take a look at some parables from Matthew and John.

Parable: The Pharisee and the Publican (Luke 18:9–14)

We can project toward persons of our own gender as illustrated in this freely translated parable of the Pharisee and the publican.

> Two men went up to the temple to pray. One of them was a good practicing churchgoer, and one a street person and an alcoholic. The good churchgoing Pharisee walked up to the front of the church and said, "I want to say, God, that I am thankful" (and then he makes the mistake) "that I am not like the rest of the people. I fast, I tithe, I pray, and I am especially thankful that I am not like that street worm back there, a liar, a thief, maybe even an adulterer. I am especially grateful for that." And he is very sincere.
>
> The fellow in back doesn't even look up. He is a publican, someone really low on the class scale. When you said "publican" in those days, you spat and kicked the wall. They were the outcasts. And this publican who couldn't lift his eyes up, said, "Oh, God, be merciful to me, a sinner." And Jesus ended by saying, "The one who went home justified in the eyes of God was the publican."

Imagine that! This fellow goes back out on the street to get some spare change for some more alcohol, and he is the one that is justified in the eyes of God. Why? Because the good churchgoer was repulsed and offended by all these negative qualities that he attributed to the publican, and he disowned any of these potentials within himself. Somehow he couldn't just overlook the publican; he had to shudder to himself and enumerate all the things this publican represented to him and then reveal his own denial that these were shameful parts of himself by thanking God that he wasn't like the publican. This good churchgoing Pharisee was not justified in the eyes of God after such a prayer because his projection prevented him from coming clean before God.

Self-righteous projection is vicious; it is a soul killer. And if we can't start owning our shadow side, we stay trapped in our dysfunctional lives, projecting onto others the very parts of ourselves that can paradoxically bring us to healing. In the process of projection, we also discount, avoid, hate, and perhaps even victimize these other people onto whom we project.

On a mass scale, projection is called prejudice. Prejudice often involves the projection of the denied, underground aspects of the majority culture onto a minority group. And the soul killing takes place both when the minority group in society has to endure being described as the rejected aspects of the majority group, and when the minority group begins to believe it is true.

For example, let's examine some of the qualities that prejudiced white people attribute to black persons in the United States. The fact that prejudiced people attribute these things to blacks does not mean that these qualities are true of blacks; they are actually the denied aspects of white culture. For example, think of the stereotypes attributed to black males by prejudiced white middle-class males: black men are less than energetic, very interested in sexuality, and are playful and carefree.

Now, think of neurotic, overdriven, white middle-class executives who don't see any way to slow down, who don't have time for lovemaking, who can't afford to get in close touch with that side of themselves, who would love to take a little more time to get in touch with nature. The traits that are attributed to black men as a negative caricature could actually be the denied yearnings of the white culture these executives come from. These yearnings may be denied and projected because they are so frightening to acknowledge. (How can a person be successful in white America and acknowledge these traits?)

Parable: The Woman Washing Jesus' Feet (Luke 7:36–50)

An example of opposite-sex projection takes place at the house of Simon, a Pharisee. Simon takes a chance with his reputation by inviting Jesus, who is a fascinating but unconventional teacher, to come in and dine with him. As Jesus is dining, a woman who is a known prostitute rushes in, grabs his feet, and begins to weep over them, kissing them and drying them with her hair. She then pours perfume on them.

> Simon is scandalized, thinking, "Surely if this man is a prophet he would know what manner of woman is *touching* him—a prostitute!"
> And Jesus said, "Simon, I have something to tell you."
> Simon says, "Speak, master."
> Jesus says, "Simon, when I came to your house tonight you didn't greet me with a kiss (a common courtesy). You kept your distance. You didn't offer to wash my feet (another common courtesy). Now, you've seen this woman here? She has been washing my feet with her tears and drying them with her hair. You did not greet me with a kiss, but she hasn't stopped kissing my feet. You didn't anoint my head with oil, but she anointed my feet with perfume."

Simon omitted the common courtesies for welcoming a guest into one's home. Perhaps he withheld such niceties to hedge against being thought to be a close friend of Jesus, which might taint his reputation with his neighbors. For whatever reason, he did not bestow upon Jesus these courtesies. No wonder he was scandalized, possibly enraged, to see them being performed by the prostitute! Perhaps Simon's anger at the woman stemmed from his longing to express passionately the deepest yearnings of his heart—both emotionally and physically. Since he didn't have this freedom, he condemned the woman (and his own rejected shadow) as unclean.

Cross-sex projections of a shadow-side characteristic can give us such intense negative or positive reactions that they are possibly the most devastating and difficult to recognize.

This parable shows more. Feet and femininity appear to be very closely associated in the Scriptures. Women are often touching Jesus' feet, the hem of his garment, grasping his legs. There's a symbolic link: the foot is in touch with the earth, which is symbolically feminine and holds profound meaning about Jesus being in touch with what is feminine.

Then Jesus said, "I tell you, that is why her many sins are forgiven, because of her great love. Little is forgiven to the one whose love is small" (Luke 7:47). Jesus affirmed feminine passion and did not devalue it. It was rather the antiseptic caution of Simon with which he had a problem.

Parable: The Speck in Our Eye (Matt. 7:3–5)

Jesus illustrates the great danger in being blind to our shadow and projecting it onto someone else in the parable of the speck in the eye. He asked the Pharisees,

Why are you so aware of the speck in your brother's eye, when indeed there is a plank in your own. You hypocrite! First, get the plank out of your own eye. And then you will see clearly enough to get the speck out of your brother's.

First of all, Jesus points out how the very trait to which we are blind is made of the same material as the trait that irritates us in someone else, but is usually bigger. This parable tells us what folk wisdom also knows: we are particularly irritated by the faults in others that illustrate our own blind side.

Parable: The Woman Caught in Adultery (John 8:3–11)

Examples of the devastating intensity of opposite-sex projection are found in other gospels as well, such as the story of the woman caught in adultery. A special way to think of it is as a dramatization of a woman's inner life, with the characters representing parts of her psyche.

The scribes and the Pharisees led a woman forward who had been caught in adultery. They made her stand there in front of everyone.

A *group* of Pharisees accuse her. The opposite-sex point of reference within a woman's psyche is often experienced as a group of men or as masculine opinions and masculine legal tradition.

"Teacher," they said to him, "this woman has been caught in the act of adultery. In the law, Moses ordered such women to be stoned. What do you have to say about the case?" (They were posing this question to trap him, so that they could have something to accuse him of.)

The woman represents everything these squeaky clean males would loathe and fear to encounter within themselves. She's a perfect object of projection— caught in the act!

Jesus recognized the psychological blindness that was being exercised: men who commit adultery are guilty of just as much wrongdoing as women. What about the man who was involved in this act of adultery? He gets off without a word. Just the woman was hauled in.

Jesus bent down and started tracing on the ground with his finger.

He touched the place where the woman was standing, the earth, which represents the feminine; Jesus was in touch with his feminine side.

When they persisted in their questioning, he straightened up and said to them, "Let the man among you who has no sin be the first to cast a stone at her."

He cut right through their projection to see if they'd own it.

A second time he bent down and wrote on the ground. Then the audience drifted away one by one, beginning with the elders.

At least the oldest knew a little.

Imagine that in a woman's psyche there is a crushing depression that seeks to devalue her, telling her that she's nothing and will never amount to anything. It seizes her, threatens and condemns her. Women who pay attention to this inner depressive process often say, "The voices seem masculine, authoritative. I can't defend myself against this. It's true, absolutely true. I'm just overwhelmed."

And yet, in the presence of Jesus, the voices begin to go away, one by one. In his presence, and in the presence of a masculinity that does not judge her, that is strong and loving, the voices start to disappear.

This left him alone with the woman, who continued to stand there before him. Jesus finally straightened up and said to her, "Woman, where did they all disappear to? Has no one condemned you?"

"No one, sir," she answered.

"I can think now." She says, "Finally the depression seems to be lifting." Somehow the woman is free.

Jesus said, "Nor do I condemn you. You may go. But from now on, avoid this sin."

The Greek word John used for sin in this story was *hamartia*, literally meaning an arrow missing the mark. In other words, the woman is told: "Don't let the passion of your heart be misdirected to this man in such a relationship. The passion of your heart is meant to be directed to an object that cannot fail your heart. Avoid this sin, or you will destroy yourself."

This story demonstrates the intensity and power of an unrecognized cross-sex projection that drove men to the brink of stoning a person to death. As soon as Jesus cut through their denial to point out the sinful nature of the men themselves, and the men owned their own guilt and sin, they walked away.

Parable: The Prodigal Son (Luke 15:11–32)

In the previous chapter, we discussed the parable of the Prodigal Son, regarding the responsible older brother and the prodigal younger brother as aspects of ourselves. At midlife the younger brother comes home, and the father throws a party for him.

In many ways, the younger brother, who represents our inner child, is also the shadow side of the older brother. The older brother is terrified of, disgusted with, and judgmental toward his younger brother. And yet the father celebrates the return of the younger brother, because the father loves him. But it is also true that the family farm needs the younger brother. The younger brother is a risk-taker, an innovator and explorer, one who sees the world and its opportunities as a gift. The older brother is systematic, organized, and (in the very best sense) conserving of and adapting what has been given to him. Both are needed for the farm: innovation of brand new ideas (based on exploration of new places) and preservation of the best of what has been developed. This rich parable may also lead us to have a welcoming, accepting attitude toward our own shadow side, and awareness of its importance and necessity for the good of the business of living.

Parable: The Sower and the Seed (Matt. 13:3–8)

Jesus presents the parable of the Sower and the Seed with a farmer sowing some seed, some of which fell on each of four different types of soil. As we saw in the previous chapter, different aspects of our psychological makeup are represented by the four soil conditions, and the seed symbolizes the Word of God that brings us to life. The second type of soil is the one that seems to relate to the lives of those who have experienced childhood enmeshment.

> Some seed fell on rocky soil where it sprang up quickly, but when the sun came up it scorched it and the plant withered, because it had no depth of root. (Matt. 13:5–6)

The sun that scorches the wheat represents adversity or challenge in our lives. As we've said, making choices and setting boundaries are difficult for those who have experienced childhood enmeshment. After being treated as extensions of our care givers, we have not established our separate identities sheltered within the invisible envelope of healthy boundaries.

When we do try to make a choice, encountering someone who either disagrees with or is opposed to our choice is like being scorched by the heat of the sun. Without any depth of root, any inner life that is distinctly our own, our resolve withers and dies. We may lose the sense of our own reasons for having made the choice, and let the opposing person overpower our preferences.

The rocky soil also represents the fact that when we go inside ourselves to develop our inner life, we are confronted with our own inner contradictions, our own darkness, our own obtuseness: both rocks and soil intermingled. We're confounded by these seeming contradictions within ourselves. Our temptation is to turn away from situations and people involving confusing contradictions because we don't like to see the nasty shadow side of ourselves. We'd rather project that onto other people.

But eventually we must face this problem of rocks in the soil because dealing with it allows us to come to awareness of who we are. In fact, the source of soil is weathered rock! In the context of working the Twelve Steps, it is facing our rocky soil through Steps Four, Five, and Six that gives us our reality and helps clarify our boundaries. Our acknowledgment of our faults and brokenness in relationship to Christ and another person brings us into relationship with ourselves. We discover we are loved in our brokenness and in our inner conflicts, and are called to bring those into harmony.

19

Redirecting Our Deep Longing for Perfect Companionship and Emotional Development to God

Many avenues guide us toward redirecting our deep longing for perfect parenting toward God. In this chapter, we will employ three of the Twelve Steps of Alcoholics Anonymous along with meditation, reflection, and journaling about the parable of the Sower and the Seed. Then we'll use some psychospiritual exercises.

The Twelve Steps: Steps Four, Five, and Six[1]

As we work Steps Four, Five, and Six of the Twelve-Step process, we are guided to focus our minds on our own reality, for the purpose of dismantling the aftermath of our childhood enmeshment experiences. Taking Steps Four through Six allows us to live with our own humanity in emotional relationship with another human being.

We've now seen that the driving force of enmeshment is projection, and nothing quite pulls the plug on projection like doing a fearless moral inventory of *ourselves*, rather than "taking someone else's inventory."

In Step Five, we acknowledge our shadow side to ourselves, God, and another human being. This helps us solve a great problem, the paradox of community. We learn how to share with others without being engulfed by them. We learn how to maintain our boundaries. Paradoxically, the Twelve-Step solution to the problem of the lack of boundaries is this: *in our shared brokenness we begin to form our boundaries in community*. In other words, our limits and our faults make us a particularly distinctive individual in need of community.

So if we share what makes us a distinct individual with someone else, and we are not rejected, then we experience acceptance at the level at which we are most individual. And we're doing it by sharing the toughest truth about ourselves.

And paradoxically we discover that we are most profoundly *like* other people at the very places we thought we were unique. The resulting feelings of closeness may be the strongest human factor in creating true spiritual community.

Paul the Apostle went through a similar experience. In his letter to the Romans, Paul lists all things that could separate us from God's love, similar to the way we list our moral inventory in Steps Four and Five. We can do our moral inventory in faith, trusting with Paul, who said, "Who shall separate us from the love of God which is in Christ Jesus? I'm convinced, nothing on heaven or on earth can separate us from the love of God which is in Christ Jesus" (Rom. 8:38–39). Acknowledging the forgiving love of God in Jesus Christ, Paul had a whole new basis of self-esteem in relating to others.

When we relate to others on the basis of our brokenness and find acceptance and forgiveness, an entirely new basis for self-esteem is created. That's why the early Christians joyfully confessed their sins to one another. Because churchgoers are today having trouble doing this in our buttoned-down, respectable society, guess who is doing it? The broken people—the alcoholics—the Twelve Steppers. They're doing what the early Christians did, confessing their sins to one another.

Then comes the Sixth Step: "We became entirely ready to have God remove all these defects of character." Step Six deals with God's respect for our boundaries in our relationship with God, for in Step Six we get ready for Jesus to change our whole lives and heal us without enmeshment. Jesus waits for *us* to become entirely ready. Jesus will respect our boundaries, will not enmesh with us, and will not even pursue a relationship with us if not freely invited.

Thus, all three Steps help free us from the trait of blaming others as we face our own shadow side. They bring us closer to a right relationship with our deep selves, with others, and with God. And they teach us that we have boundaries as we face and admit both the positive and dysfunctional limits of our lives.

The Lessons in the Parables

Review, in the previous chapter, the comments about how these three parables illustrate the problem of enmeshment: the Woman Caught in Adultery, the Prodigal Son, and the Sower and the Seed. The following questions might help you apply these comments to your own life. Write your responses in your journal.

The Woman Caught in Adultery

1. When you are depressed, what recurring thoughts, if any, go through your mind (the way the voices condemned the woman caught in adultery)? In other words, what do the condemning voices in your head tell you?

2. To what objects have you been directing your need for love? A spouse, a child, a parent, an organization, a job? Are these objects ultimately satisfying?

The Prodigal Son

1. What shadow side trait or traits have appeared in your life recently that have been difficult to welcome and accept?

Example: A. controlling my teenagers

B. criticizing the people who work under me about their office procedures

2. After meditating on each trait listed above, write out any thoughts that occur to you about how you might behave if you were able to welcome and accept the trait.

Example: A. I might be able to let my kids experience the consequences of their actions instead of trying to protect them by making their choices for them.

B. I might limit my comments to describing only insufficient results, asking for cooperation in finding the solution without attacking anyone's procedures.

3. Try out each of the behaviors you have listed above, then describe what happened.

Example: A. I told my sixteen-year-old son I would not nag him about going to bed or getting up any more. He decided to stay up reading a detective novel. My husband and I left for work the next morning without making sure he got up. He woke up late, missed his ride to school, had to call a cab, pay for the fare, and face the penalty for being late.

B. I presented two problems at a staff meeting and was delighted by the resulting suggestions. Some of them were better than what I thought we should do!

The Sower and the Seed

1. Make headings at the top of two columns on a fresh page in your journal: Choice and Opposition. In the first column, list any choices or decisions you made that met opposition from someone else. In the second column describe the opposition you encountered.

Example:

Choice	Opposition
A. To see a certain movie	Spouse wanted to stay home and read
B. To visit Carlsbad Caverns	Kids wanted to visit their cousins at the beach

2. List any inner conflicts the previous step may be suggesting, but that you can't quite own just yet.

Example: A. How much has pleasing my spouse interfered with my own necessary recreation?

B. How do I use authority in the family? Is my family "child-driven"?

3. After meditating on each opposition listed in step 1, and each inner conflict listed in step 2, write any thoughts that occur to you about how you might behave if you were able to integrate these inner conflicts.

Example: A. I am taking more responsibility for my own self-care. My spouse will not know my needs or preferences unless I state them.

B. My relationship with my children sometimes evokes feelings in me of what it felt like to be a child their age. How can these feelings guide me in my use of authority?

4. Try out one of the behaviors you have listed above, then describe what happened.

Psychospiritual Exercises

PROJECTION WITHDRAWAL

A psychological exercise for dealing with the pain of having experienced enmeshment is called Projection Withdrawal. This exercise can open up deep possibilities for personal growth, but it is difficult.

In this exercise, we are guided to learn from bothersome characteristics and behaviors that we see in others. Faith in a Higher Power allows us to face the proposition that what we think is objective psychological reality in our relationships may be, in fact, a projection. The process can be quite painful and paradoxical. But as Jesus pointed out in Matthew, we have an immediate social opportunity for withdrawing projections: the most rapid method for withdrawing projection is to love our enemies. To the extent that we can learn to love our enemies, we will be able to love the "enemy" within ourselves (Matt. 5:44).

What to Do

Shadow Projection

1. When you are very upset by someone else's behavior, describe in your journal the encounter with the person. (Tell what happened between you.)
2. Make a list of the qualities of the person that upset you.
3. Separating the qualities from the person, meditate on the qualities you have just described. Put the actual encounter with the person who has the qualities out of your mind. Try to discover how these qualities may be operating in your own life and whether they are a reality or only a potential. Describe what you discover in the space below the list of qualities.

Example

1. *Description of Encounter:*   Last week I drove from my office to the south part of town. I was racing to get there because I was behind schedule. My route took me past a jogging trail, where I saw a bronzed jogger striding majestically past the blooming flowers. I made a joke about a running addiction and thanked God I'm not an empty-headed jock like that.

2. *Irritating Qualities:*   Fitness, tan, strides majestically, resembles Adonis, exercising during working hours.

3. *How These Qualities Apply to Me:*   I don't exercise well, if at all, and I hurt myself when I do. I'm not in shape.

Example

1. *Description of Encounter:*   I was at the airport getting ready to get on a shuttle flight, thinking "B-a-a-a" like all the other sheep getting ready to be herded on board. At the other gate I saw a well-tanned couple with tennis rackets on their way to the United flight to go to Hawaii. Before I realized what was happening, I felt a flush of irritation and smug superiority, and I thanked God I don't lead the existentially empty life of the decadent rich.

2. *Irritating Qualities:* Suntanned, tennis rackets, taking a trip to Hawaii, had enough money to take time off from work for an expensive (by my standards) vacation.

3. *How These Qualities Apply to Me:* I have difficulty knowing how to have joy in life or recreation. My sarcasm and irritation at them is really about me, not about them.

Example

1. *Description of Encounter:* I broke up a loud angry argument between my kids. I found myself getting very upset that they have become this angry and are not working together harmoniously.

2. *Irritating Qualities:* Open expression of anger at a family member, selfishness, loudness.

3. *How These Qualities Apply to Me:* I am afraid to express anger in communicating my needs with other family members. My own suppressed anger seems dangerous and destructive to me; I am afraid I will be rejected if I express anger directly.

These are examples of shadow projection. In the response to the images of exercise presented by the male jogger and recreation presented by the couple, the language in the examples sounds a lot like the righteous pharisee who thanked God he wasn't like the sinner on the back row. Breaking up an angry fight may get us into uncomfortable proximity to our own suppressed anger toward family members. We might attempt to overcontrol our children's anger as a way to "put a lid" on our own.

OPPOSITE-SEX PROJECTION

Paying attention to our sexual attractions provides much information about where we need to grow next. By doing these "internal checklists" for negative and positive projections, we can become much more aware of the internal reality we project onto others, and we are thereby freed to respond to our projections as personal growth areas, instead of blindly overreacting to other people.

What to Do

When you are sexually attracted to someone you know, or to a stranger you happen to see, make a list of the qualities of that person. There are two ways to do this.

1. If the person is someone you know, write out the attractive attributes that you believe this person has. These can be physical, mental, emotional, spiritual, personal, occupational—whatever the attributes are.

2. If the person is a stranger, you can use a process called "active imagination" in which you construct the person's image in your mind and ask the image to tell you its qualities. Or, as with someone familiar, you can just describe the qualities that attract you to the person.

Example

Person: Barber student at barber college.

Qualities: Youthful, carefree, playful, way-out style of dress, carried jam box.

How These Qualities Apply to My Next Growth Area: After talking to her image with the "active imagination" process, I learned she represented fun to me. I had been driving myself to finish an extra work project and needed to do something fun for myself. I was attracted to her personification of fun.

NOTE

1. See Appendix A for all twelve Steps.

Healing from Abuse

20

The Unmet Need for Perfect Power and Freedom

An effect of having experienced in childhood situations in which a care giver abused his or her power over us seems to be that when we as adults encounter what we perceive to be opposition or constraints, we sometimes misuse our own personal power. This stems from our yearning for perfect power, vitality, and freedom. We wonder, are we ever really going to be free to express our own individuality? We seem to want to be able to say, "I did it my way!"

Not only do we experience this cry for freedom at a personal level, but this ethic also dominates the United States. We are used to saying that the United States is the "land of the free." Liberty seems to be our highest value. We believe in the individual having lots of liberty and initiative. We would apparently rather suffer the abuses of liberty than the abuses of authority.

In this country, the development of initiative is strongly rewarded, so this section speaks to ourselves as a nation as well as to us as individuals. How do we handle ourselves as free individuals in this world?

We seek to develop our own personal power and freedom to the point where we can control our destiny and get ahead, and we are often frustrated whenever our success is thwarted by life's events, our own limits, or apparent interference from others. One positive outcome of this pain and frustration is learning to develop greater awareness of a power greater than ourselves, what Christians call the power of the Holy Spirit in our lives. By increasing our ability to cooperate with the Holy Spirit rather than trying to ignore, replace, or contradict this power, we can find more serenity and satisfaction with life the way it is, and with our part in it. Disappointments are tempered by an awareness that the reason for the disappointment may bring us unexpected compensation or may have helped us avoid an unforeseen disaster.

As we have seen, abuse occurs when one person directly hurts another. Some people have defined anything that is dysfunctional as abusive, but here the term is limited to direct injury.

Abuse, however it occurs, is about power; it is not specifically about the vehicle of the abuse (such as sex or money). We believe people often misunderstand sexual abuse. While it is certainly about sexual violation, it primarily concerns the misuse of power in a trust relationship. This particular misuse of power causes great damage interpersonally; it disempowers people on a most intimate level.

Our natural inclination for playful trial-and-error learning is the healthy gift that our yearning for personal power and freedom brings us. But when this yearning is misdirected, it has a shadow side. When ruled by the shadow side, a person who encounters obstacles or is thwarted does not just lose or get mad; this person gets even. In other words, when distressed, he or she hurts someone else. Such a person, when frustrated, can become a psychological "terrorist," someone who strikes out beyond normal moral limits, and who worries other people with the question of when he or she is going to strike next.

We in America seem to be quite fascinated with terrorism; perhaps this is because people are almost always fascinated with their shadow-side characteristics. We as a nation at times act in a manner that may seem to the rest of the world to be random and militaristic. Accusing other people of being terrorists and attempting to snuff terrorism out may illustrate the behavior we may have regarding shadow-side projection as explored in the previous chapter. Of course, we need to keep trying to counteract the behavior of terrorists, but we also need to look at the inner message our fascination with terrorism holds for *us*.

Preconversion Saul was somewhat of a terrorist as he tried to eradicate Christians. He may have been frightened or angered by his own yearning for the fulfillment and peace Christians were finding in their lives. Saul was well trained in the Jewish law, and yet seemed to be driven to persecute Christians, perhaps because he was battling within himself a realization that he could not follow the law faithfully. The freedom from legalism that he both feared and yearned for was personified in the upstart sect of Christians. Before Saul came to terms with what was within himself, he dealt with his anger and fear by attempting to eliminate Christians—only to be further confounded by the courage and conviction with which they died. Saul's behavior is a good example of the misuse of personal power, and it mirrors the way we may persecute others onto whom we project our shadow side when we are not in proper contact with our inner yearning or with the Holy Spirit.

21

God's Proper Use of Power: The Gospel of Mark

The Gospel of Mark, the shortest of the four Gospels, addresses the problem of our abuse of power. This gospel is more concerned with action than with teaching. Almost a quarter of the story describes the action of the passion and the death of Jesus. The storytelling is vivid, urgent, "on the go." The writer immediately plunges into the active ministry of Jesus, who was *Jehosua*, God's warrior, savior of his people.

Mark's Gospel shows Jesus' proper use of power, summed up in these four powerful actions (ones with which we seem to have great difficulty):

1. forgiveness,
2. owning one's own imperfection and fallibility,
3. laying down one's life, and
4. fighting evil.

There seem to be two strong themes in Mark's gospel:

1. Jesus working wonderful cures, and more importantly,
2. Jesus driving out devils, attacking and vanquishing the power of Satan.

Both have to do with the breakthrough power of the cross.

Mark describes Jesus' dealings with people who resist what he is trying to tell them. Jesus plays a very dangerous political game, while at the same time waging spiritual warfare against the kingdom of Satan. Mark's Gospel includes many confrontations with demons and driving out of these forces. People who work in the field of mental health can appreciate this driving out of demons, in particular the people who work in chemical dependency.

In Jesus' time, an uncontrollable impulse was described as "demonic," believed to be due to a foreign hostile spirit within the person. These seemingly independent, destructive, "self-defeating" behaviors are often seen today as linked with intergenerational denial and dysfunction, which seem foreign to our conscious minds and wills, but which impel us nonetheless toward self-destructive behavior. Whether one postulates an objective demonic "personality" or the destructive power of intergenerational dysfunction, using the adjective "demonic" to describe these behaviors seems very accurate.

Jesus, in his contest with evil, exercises power that is not abusive; it works for good. One particular characteristic of Jesus is that he never lets evil name him. He names and silences evil spirits; he will not let them cry out. At one point, a man with an unclean spirit appeared in the synagogue, and shrieked,

> . . . I know who you are, the holy one of God.
> Jesus rebuked him sharply, "Be quiet. Come out of the man." (Mark 1:23–25)

At first it seems strange that Jesus would want to prevent demons from naming him if he wants his message to be known. In that society, however, to name something meant you had power over it. Adam named all creatures and thus was master of creation. Even more important, in Hebrew society no one was permitted to say the holy name of God; God was the One who could not be grasped or circumscribed by a name. If Jesus permitted evil to name him, he indicated it had power over him. But in reality he had power over evil. He named it. He would not permit it to name him.

The Cross

Mark's Gospel addresses the deep yearning for perfect power and freedom in our lives. Mark describes how Jesus answers this yearning with the paradox of the cross, demonstrating a willingness to endure terrible suffering for the sake of greater life, a courageous and free sacrifice of self-will, to open up to the power of God.

In First Corinthians, Paul says, "But we preach Christ crucified—a stumbling block to Jews, and an absurdity to Gentiles; but to those who are called, Jews and Greeks alike, Christ the power of God and the wisdom of God" (1 Cor. 1:23–24).

It was a great paradox in those days that a cross could be linked with the power of God. A cross was anything but power. It was a humiliating form of execution.

It was so horrible that the crucifix was not used as a devotional object until about the sixth century A.D. Before that time, people used different images of Jesus in worship, principally that of the Good Shepherd. Having a crucifix in a church in those days would be as shocking as having an electric chair as a devotional object in a church today.

Jesus said, "The reason my Father loves me is that I lay down my life—only to take it up again. No one takes it from me, but I lay it down of my own accord. I have authority to lay it down and authority to take it up again. This command I received from my father" (John 10:17–18). Jesus showed us the proper use of personal power by freely laying down his life on a cross for others.

Once Jesus said something truly astonishing, "But I, when I am lifted up from the earth, will draw all men to myself" (John 12:32). He was referring, as people reflected on this, to his crucifixion, being lifted upright after being nailed to a cross.

Picture Christ's death on the cross as Jesus receiving the projection of our shadow sides. In the crucifixion, he can be seen as the object of all of our self-hate projected on him. Because we find it very hard to face our own shadow characteristics in ourselves—all of our self-loathing, despair, self-hate, self-contempt—we projected them on Jesus, who was killed as if he were this most vile outcast. In this way, he draws all people to himself. ". . . The Son of Man has not come to be served but to serve—to give his life in ransom for many" (Mark 10:45).

One writer said that the crucifix reminds us that the God we worship became a man to give us the courage to be fully human. We often use religion to *escape* our human shadow side. But Jesus experienced humanity to its very darkest depths. He has plunged into the shadow ahead of us, and invites us to follow him to our own cross. "He summoned the crowd with his disciples and said to them: 'If a man wishes to come after me, he must deny his very self, take up his cross and follow in my steps. Whoever would preserve his life will lose it, but whoever loses his life for my sake and the gospel's will preserve it' " (Mark 8:34–35).

Today, we continue to need saving from our righteous rejection of our shadow characteristics. Through Jesus' crucifixion and resurrection, God offers us the paradoxical promise of renewal by following Christ into crucifying shadow aspects of ourselves.

Our Deepest Need Answered

Our deep yearning for power and freedom is answered by Mark's Gospel, which presents a picture of God in action, healing sickness and overcoming evil. Mark's

Gospel addresses the pain of having experienced childhood abuse directly, offering a clear picture of God's ultimate power—the death and resurrection of Jesus Christ. We can learn to embrace our own humanity and brokenness, and begin to allow God's power to work in us, bringing us to freedom and the ultimate satisfaction for this inner yearning.

22

Amazing Stories: God's Action in and Through Our Lives

Because Mark's Gospel contains fewer of Jesus' teachings or parables, we will look at parables from other Scriptures for illustrations of God's proper use of power.

Parable: The Weeds and Wheat (Matt. 13:24–30)

He proposed to them another parable: "The reign of God may be likened to a man who sowed good seed in his field. While everyone was asleep, his enemy came and sowed weeds through his wheat, and then made off. When the crop began to mature and yield grain, the weeds made their appearance as well. The owner's slaves came to him and said, 'Sir, where are the weeds coming from?'

"He answered, 'I see an enemy's hand in this.'

"His slaves said to him, 'Do you want us to go out and pull them up?'

" 'No,' he replied, 'pull up the weeds and you might take the wheat along with them. Let them grow together until harvest; then at harvest time I will order the harvesters, First collect the weeds and bundle them up to burn, then gather the wheat into my barn.' "

A gardener once shared an interesting fact that shows how this parable relates to the recovery process. She said, "I've noticed something as I garden. You know how we say a child is 'growing up like a weed'? Well, things also grow *down* like a weed. Weeds send their roots deeper than the cultivated plants. It seems that the deeper weed roots bring up moisture and nutrients in the soil to the root level of cultivated plants that these cultivated plants couldn't reach."

We, too, have psychological weeds entangled at the root or subsoil level of our unconscious. We never quite get rid of the weeds, so recovery is a lifelong process. The weeds are not completely rooted out because they have a purpose: they bring us a gift. These weeds, the instinctual, smarmy side that we fear, actually bring us nutrients (pain, insight, and so forth), inform us about the direction our recovery needs to take, and provide vital information that we could get no other way. The powerlessness we sometimes experience in confronting our lifelong "weeds" teaches us about the true source of power that can change our lives: the cross of Jesus Christ. Even though psychological weeds create problems in our lives, they also bring us elements necessary for our recovery. This is an example of the paradoxical power of facing our shadow side.

Jesus said,

> I solemnly assure you, unless the grain of wheat falls to the earth and dies, it remains just a grain of wheat. But if it dies, it produces much fruit. (John 12:24)

The grain of wheat falling to the earth gives us an image of the necessary suffering in human life. Life can be personally and impersonally punitive. However, what we first experience as simple punishment can sometimes later be seen as the occasion for spiritual growth. Jesus points out that what we experience as abusive in life can be transformed into the conditions that strip away old defenses and prepare us for a greater life. This is necessary because what we had first thought was real and secure in our lives is often part of our projection and denial, our protective "husk" that must be shed. This is similar to Erikson's paradoxical scheme of human development; we must shed (or sacrifice) what we thought was our greatest strength in order to experience new growth. And suffering often causes us to confront our denial and dysfunction at each stage of our development.

Bible Story: Peter Dealing with His Betrayal of Jesus

In the final story of Peter and Jesus, we learn how Jesus properly uses his power to deal with us and our shadow side when we encounter him. Peter must deal with his own shadow side: he who boasted to Jesus, "if all abandoned you, I would die for you," has himself miserably betrayed Jesus.

Earlier Jesus had said, "Satan is going to sift you like wheat, Simon. Just be ready" (Luke 22:31). So if Peter, the Rock, got sifted, why do we think we can do better than he? Of course our lives will get unmanageable!

Peter's betrayal has turned him inside out, particularly at the central point of his moral self-esteem. He thought himself incapable of betrayal. He wandered around after the resurrection, wondering what to do with himself. He had even seen Jesus, but didn't know what to do. So, perhaps remembering that he first saw Jesus near a boat when he was fishing, he told his nearby friends that he was going out to fish, and they went with him. After a night of fishing without catching anything, they once again saw Jesus standing on the shore at daybreak. After this third encounter with Jesus, in which they caught fish, cooked them, and ate together, Jesus began an interaction with Peter that seems to be very similar to a healing-of-memories ceremony. He knew Peter had denied him, had abused his power by failing to be counted as a follower of Christ after having sworn that he would never deny him. He knew Peter was miserable, and needed to be healed from the pain of this memory.

> When they had eaten their meal, Jesus said to Simon Peter, "Simon, son of John, do you love me more than these?"
> "Yes, Lord," he said. "You know that I love you."
> At which Jesus said, "Feed my lambs."
> A second time he put his question, "Simon, son of John, do you love me?"

Simon might have thought, "You are a cruel one, Jesus. You are going to do this in front of everybody? Don't you understand? I am the leader you appointed. Don't shame me in front of them." But Jesus had asked again, "Do you love me, Simon?"

> Peter said, "You know that I love you."
> Jesus replied, "Tend my sheep."
> A third time, Jesus asked him, "Simon, son of John, do you love me?"

The third time is a charm; it undoes the three denials.

> Peter was hurt because he had asked him a third time "Do you love me?" So he said to him: "Lord, you know everything. You know well that I love you."
> Jesus said to him, "Feed my sheep."
> [He went on.] "I tell you solemnly: as a young man you fastened your belt and went about as you pleased; but when you are older you will stretch out your hands, and another will tie you fast and carry you off against your will."
> (What he said indicated the sort of death by which Peter was to glorify God.) When Jesus had finished speaking he said to him, "Follow me" (John 21:15–19).

In other words, the first half of your life you go around as you please, or so you think. But in the second half of your life, all of your commitments, all of your particular circumstances, even your body binds you and carries you off in a direction you don't want to go.

And then Jesus said, "Follow me." This is what he says to us on this way of the cross. But in this process, he broke Peter open like an egg and healed his inner pain. This is what happens to us and our shame when we encounter Christ: He gently breaks us open and heals us of levels we thought were impenetrable or in no need of healing.

Parable: The Good Samaritan

The parable of the Good Samaritan has multiple levels, one of which relates to the abuse of power. (To review the parable, refer to chapter 11 or to Luke 10:25–27.)

A human being leaves his or her defenses to begin a necessary journey "down" to Jericho (a thousand feet below sea level), the ancient fortress that guarded the Promised Land. But the person is attacked by robbers, stripped, beaten, and left for dead. The person encounters abuse on the journey, and is injured, almost fatally. In this broken, dysfunctional condition, no one wants to touch the person except the Samaritan, an outcast.

This parable offers a pointed illustration of our attitudes toward brokenness in ourselves and others. We often do not appreciate how we have abused power and truly hurt others until we have been victimized ourselves. *Then* we are sensitive to powerlessness, brokenness, and how we might have contributed to it.

Parable: The Sower and the Seed (Matt. 13:3–8)

The farmer sowed his seed, and some of it fell on each of four soil conditions. (To review this parable, refer to chapter 14 or to Matt. 13:3–8.) The third of these soil conditions Jesus names is this: some seed fell among thorns and the plant sprang up, but the thorns sprang up with it and the thorns choked the plant.

As mentioned previously, the soil conditions can represent psychological aspects of ourselves, and the seed represents the Word of God. The problems of life represented by the seed falling among thorns have to do with matters above the soil, or external to ourselves. This contrasts with the problems of life represented by rocky soil, which have to do with matters of the inner life. This is an important difference between the effects of abuse and the effects of enmeshment.

The thorns can represent encounters we have with external circumstances or other people, with roots that extend to our own inner life. When we have experienced abuse in childhood—harsh or unjust punishment—the consequence for us is the loss of safety and freedom, or difficulty finding a safe place or enough space for trial-and-error learning. Now, as adults, dealing with people or circumstances in which we can't have our own way seems to us to choke off the products of our labor and our own reality. Our reality is not completely overrun, as in the effect of enmeshment, but we are hurt externally.

We are also affected at the root level, where the wheat roots are entangled with those of the thorns. When our lives produce both thorns and wheat, we must develop sensitivity and awareness of when we have injured other people. We must grapple with the danger of confusing God's will (coming from the seed) with our will (coming from the thorns) in the world of action. In addition, there is our potential to misuse God's gift and misuse our power and freedom. That is why Christians pray, ". . . and deliver us from evil." It is precisely when we have attained power and freedom that we are most tempted to use it simply for ourselves. Yet another effect of having experienced abuse in childhood is that we face this problem of proper conduct, of real action outside of ourselves. Learning the proper use of power and freedom is the key task of recovery from abuse.

23

Redirecting Our Deep Longing for Perfect Power and Freedom to God

There are many approaches we can use to redirect to God our deep longing for power and freedom. In this chapter, we will cover three of the Twelve Steps developed by Alcoholics Anonymous, also some meditation, reflection, and journaling on the parable of the Sower and the Seed, and some psychospiritual exercises.

The Twelve Steps: Steps Seven, Eight, and Nine[1]

The entire set of Twelve Steps was created because of alcoholics' acting out in abusive ways. Thus, all the steps perhaps deal more with the aftermath of the childhood experience of abuse than with neglect, enmeshment, or abandonment. The process of working the steps helps people change behaviorally, people who have abused alcohol, drugs, other people, and their own bodies, minds, and moral values.

In particular, however, Steps Seven, Eight, and Nine deal with reversing abuse, because they show us that when God takes away our shortcomings, God not only refrains from abusing us but also brings us into God's process of reconciliation by leading us through the process of forgiving people and making amends.

These three steps are dubbed the "action steps." They model for us the proper use of power, involving (as Jesus spelled out in Mark) forgiveness, owning our own imperfection and fallibility, turning to God for healing, going out of our way to make restitution, and fighting the evil (character defects) within us.

The Seventh Step is, "Humbly asked God to remove all these shortcomings." In this step, we ask God to heal all our character defects, which in effect states that we know we çannot do it without God. We have been prepared by the Sixth Step, in which we experienced that God will not enmesh us, and that God will wait for us to become entirely ready for God to act for good in our lives. Now, in the Seventh Step, we see that God will not abuse us either. We humbly ask God to remove our shortcomings—and then we see that God does not use power to rip away any attitudes, behaviors, or feelings to which we still cling. God takes only what we will release.

Step Eight is, "Made a list of all persons we have harmed and became willing to make amends to them all." In this step, we move from admitting generally that we have abused our power to listing specific instances of it—who, what, where, how, and so on. Making amends is the precise reversal of abuse.

Step Nine is, "Made direct amends to such people wherever possible except when to do so would injure them or others." The step cautions us not to abuse someone in the process of making amends. When a direct amends would injure someone, we seek to find an indirect method of carrying out this step. This is very similar to what a converted Christian is to do: to forgive and make amends.

These three steps show us power in action—really doing things in the world. They bring us to accountability and the possibility of forgiveness, including self-forgiveness. This two-pronged forgiveness is the way community problems get solved, and is actually the experience of the Holy Spirit, who is the source of the proper use of power and shows us how to get things done in the world of relationships.

Lessons from the Scriptures

Review the comments in chapter 22 about how the two parables, the Weeds and Wheat, and the Sower and the Seed, each illustrate the problem of abuse. Apply them to your own life by responding in your journal to the following questions.

The Weeds and the Wheat

1. Describe any psychological "weeds" in your life that have come to your awareness in your recovery journey, the "instinctual, smarmy" side of yourself that hampers your relationships.

   Example: I am so forgetful about car maintenance. I didn't change the oil and I really hurt the engine this time! I try to remember, but I always seem to pay attention to everything else first!

2. Describe how these aspects of yourself have actually helped you with renewed energy or insight to move forward with your recovery.

Example: My physical neglect of my car parallels my physical neglect of myself. I would rather be free of paying attention to my car. But this physically "weedy" part of me reminds me to take care of my real "vehicle" in life: my body. So, the struggle to remember to care for my car has a great gift: it keeps me conscious of the requirement to care for my body.

The Sower and the Seed

1. What thorns have you encountered in your life, external circumstances that have interfered with your recovery?
2. In what ways are the thorny parts of your own personality (self-will at the root level) choking off the fruits of recovery and harming yourself or others?

Psychospiritual Exercises

The exercise offered here is designed to approach the healing of our own inner woundedness resulting from the experience of childhood abuse.

Healing of Memories

This exercise helps us form a relationship with God in the presence of a memory that is full of pain, guiding us to seek empowerment and healing by redirecting our deep longing for power and freedom to God. We go back into our memories, accompanied by God, and preferably in the presence of someone we trust (perhaps a minister or counselor trained in healing of memories, or someone who knows about this process).[2]

This process adds something to what we may already be doing in working on the painful memory with a therapist. Often, a very real problem with therapy is termination; it's over at a certain point. You deal with the issues, and then you leave the relationship. It's similar to leaving home, and that's the way it's supposed to be with a good counselor. The client is encouraged to get to the end of it, and to go away with new insights and tools with which to cope.

Yet, as we have seen, our hearts yearn for constant relationship. An important aspect of the healing of memories process is developing a relationship with God, who does not go away. So even after the end of our relationship with a counselor, minister, or close friend who was with us as we worked on the painful memory, we retain and continue the relationship we are developing with God.

What to Do

If you have upsetting emotions, compulsive behaviors, or obsessive ideas, these may be fueled by a painful unconscious memory. Here is a four-step process for discovering and healing such painful unconscious memories.

1. *Recognizing Disturbances:* Put yourself into a quiet state and name the disturbance, the upsetting emotion, compulsive behavior, or obsessive idea. Imagine God with you as you try to locate the memory that is fueling the disturbance. If the image of God or Jesus is too harsh or frightening for you right now, imagine a trusted, loving friend who could represent God's love. By getting centered in this way, you can find a safe place to receive the memory image.

You may find it helpful to imagine being in a private theater. Imagine you are seated beside Jesus or God or a trusted friend. You and God or the loving friend are the only two in the audience part of the theater.

2. *Receiving the Memory Image:* Pray humbly to God to give you an image or memory that is associated with the disturbing thought, feeling, or behavior. Remain in quiet prayer until a memory comes. A memory or image, in just the right "dose" from the unconscious, will usually surface.

If you were using the theater image in step 1, now imagine that there are curtains covering the stage, and behind the curtains there is action going on. You can see the bumping against the curtains as the play scenery gets put into place. When the curtains open in your imagination, the scene that you see will often be a scene that will help you remember something that is connected to what you've been feeling.

Another helpful image is that of sitting with God or a trusted friend next to a deep natural pool of clear water, waiting for the memory to float up from the bottom. When the memory is released from your unconscious mind, it is reflected in the still, smooth surface of the pool.

Next, describe in your journal the memory or scene that has surfaced for you. Although writing a description of it is not necessary for the exercise to be effective, we make this suggestion for those who find writing a helpful tool in memory work.

3. *Active Imagination:* Accompanied by God or your trusted friend, go into the memory that has appeared, using all your inner senses. Feel the feelings; listen to

the conversations and look at the activity. Talk with persons or elements in the memory. Listen for any response. Talk with God or your friend about these events, or watch God or your friend interact with people or objects in the memory.

If you are using the theater image, in this step look at the scene from your life. You may see yourself as part of the scene. You can listen to the characters, watch what happens, even interrupt the action and ask them to explain why they did what they did. You can ask Jesus or your trusted friend why the characters did it. Jesus or your friend can go up on stage and talk to people. You can watch all this as it happens.

Describe in your journal the active imagination you have done with this memory. List any questions you asked and the answers you received, any actions or comments made by God or the person whom you trust who is with you in your imagination, or any other pertinent aspects of this stage of your visualization.

4. *Healing:* Interacting with the memory allows you to understand events in context, from others' points of view, and this can help you to forgive, or to be able to pray for the other people involved in the memory. When the painful event originally occurred, the memory is often repressed in all its childhood, egocentric intensity. Entering the memory helps to "contextualize" the event, to appreciate others' motives, to integrate the memory into consciousness, and to heal.

Psychological healing involves consciously absorbing the painful emotions associated with the memory, and understanding what the memory means for you. Such healing brings us a freeing of our present life from the disturbance of thought, emotion, or behavior that was fueled by the painful memory, and a deepening of our faith and love in the healing God, who, unlike a human counselor, need not leave us at the termination of therapy.

It is important to note here that there is a crucial difference between understanding another person's point of view in this exercise and *excusing* the abusive part of the memory, rather than forgiving it. By merely excusing, we fail to acknowledge that what happened was abusive and painful to us. We then adopt an attitude of, "Well, he or she couldn't help it because of these circumstances, so I wasn't injured." By contrast, in the forgiveness process we *own our pain, acknowledge the abuse, then release it in forgiveness.*

Dennis and Matthew Linn have astutely observed that forgiveness involves processing *all* the emotions of the grieving process: denial, anger, bargaining, depression, and acceptance. Understood this way, moving into anger out of denial *is* forgiveness; moving from diffuse anger into pointed bargaining (and sometimes confrontation) *is* forgiveness; moving from bargaining into the depressing powerlessness of our wound, and yielding to the power of God to heal and transform us *is* forgiveness, and finally accepting the life transformation that healing involves—all of this is forgiveness.[3]

1. At what stage do you seem to be with this painful memory at this time (anger, bargaining, depression, acceptance and forgiveness)? (Denial is omitted because if the memory has surfaced for healing, you have already come out of denial about it.)
2. Describe the reasons you chose this stage.
3. As we eventually pass through these stages of forgiveness with the original memory, we may then begin the healing of memories process anew, asking for a deeper memory, as part of our faith journey. As you move through each stage in the process of forgiveness, record in your journal your thoughts and feelings along the way.

NOTES

1. See Appendix A for all twelve Steps as developed by Alcoholics Anonymous.
2. If you would like more information about this process, see Dennis and Matthew Linn, *Healing of Memories* (New York: Paulist Press, 1974), and Dennis and Matthew Linn, *Healing Life's Hurts* (New York: Paulist Press, 1978). These books provide even more detailed directions and exercises.
3. Dennis and Matthew Linn, *Healing Life's Hurts* (New York: Paulist Press, 1978).

Healing from Abandonment

24

The Unmet Need for Perfect Meaning and Perspective

Experiencing childhood abandonment may lead to our having difficulty sensing our own purpose and meaning for our lives, and perhaps also difficulty with living life in the framework of our chronological age. We may be immature or overmature for our age. For example, a thirty-year-old secretary may break into childish tantrums when someone thwarts her or into tears when her boss requests her to do something over. A fifty-year-old executive may be childishly irresponsible about keeping track of where things are, relying on his wife, secretary, and others to find things for him. A teenager may show adult maturity when asked to care for younger siblings, but may also lose touch with the spontaneity and playfulness characteristic of teenage years.

Due to childhood abandonment, we may have little or no ability to recognize accurately our own physical limits (such as how much weight we can lift or how much food is enough) or physical condition (such as when we're tired or hungry) or emotional condition (such as when we're angry or in pain). We may have difficulty with our thinking, including problem solving, forming opinions, and making decisions. We may have trouble with our behavior, with doing the right thing for the occasion or at the right time (such as working when we need to work, relaxing when we need to rest, going to the doctor, recognizing when our children need our attention and giving it to them, responding to an invitation, sending a thank-you note, being on time).

As we seek healing, however, we can begin to turn from trying to find the meaning or purpose of our lives in behaviors, achievements, substances, or material possessions. We can channel this deep need for meaning and purpose toward greater perception of the Holy Trinity dwelling within us, working in the unfolding of our life and in the rest of the world. We can thus learn to tolerate our disappointment better when our children, professional goals, retirement income or other parts of our lives don't turn out as we would have liked.

A Point of Clarification in Using Jung's Psychological Tools

Carl Jung offered many valuable tools for looking deeply at the human psyche in our own personal struggles. I (Richard Grant) encountered a problem, however, in my initial misunderstanding and misuse of a term Jung called the Self.[1]

Jung proposed that there is a dynamic principle operating deep within us that works to bring us to wholeness, or sanity. In this wholeness or sanity we are aware of distinct parts, like thoughts from the conscious mind, images from the unconscious mind, and emotions, that work together in harmony. The dynamic principle that organizes all of these parts Jung called the "Self." He said that in his experience with the dreams and artistic productions of Christian people, there was no observable difference between the Self and the image of Christ, and that he believed the image of Christ to be a symbol of the Self.

That is where I got into difficulty, because Jung's statement could be interpreted to mean, "the experience of Christ comes entirely from within a person's reality." In this interpretation, Jung's theory of the Self does not require an historical, scriptural revelation of Christ from outside the Self, but only personal introspection.

My first understanding of this led me into a subtle form of spiritual self-sufficiency that needed no community-tested revelation or salvation from outside myself—from God. This suggestion of self-sufficiency may seem attractive to many people, but I believe it can lead to a kind of self-centered, spiritual individualism that eliminates the need for an external, personal relationship to God and to other people. Such a use of Jung's tools deemphasizes revelation, tradition, and involvement in a Christian worshiping community.

As I matured, however, my experience of the Twelve Steps and of Christianity convinced me that we need others to mirror our unreality (and reality), and as guides and friends when we get into the deeper recesses of our brokenness as we move toward healing. I began to understand that the great difference between spiritual self-sufficiency and Christianity is this: Christianity says that there is a revelation, an action of God in history called salvation that is real and experienced. This contrasts with a view that doesn't expect salvation, believing only in *self*-help and *self*-revelation.

Actually, Jung's ideas and tools do not *supplant* revelation; in fact, they *confirm* the revelation of God's saving plan by offering some psychological contact points with the spiritual realm. Believing in God's revelation does not mean we cannot use Jung's ideas and tools for psychological and spiritual growth. By recognizing the organizing, healing principle within us as the Logos, we can use Jung's tools to help us become aware of this process, particularly in any psychotherapy involving dreams. We can direct our unmet need for perfect meaning and perspective to God by experiencing that Jesus Christ is *really* operating in our lives, bringing us to healing, and "the gates of hell" (the negative potentials of archetypal reality) shall not prevail against us (Matt. 16:19).

I came to believe that it is through this organizing and integrating principle, which Jung saw as the Self, that we encounter Jesus Christ, the Logos, at work in our unconscious.

Our Role Is a Response, Not Simply Our Own Initiative

There is a point at which our initiative in the Twelve Steps finds its limits. The Twelve Steps emphasize that we humans establish a relationship with God, open ourselves up to God, and that God takes action in our lives. At the beginning, our sense of human initiative is very appealing to those of us who value self-sufficiency.

But there can be too strong an emphasis on human action in this program, almost as though *we're* making the recovery happen for ourselves. In our culture, we promote the concept that all of us have the freedom and opportunity to earn our way to the top, and that, in fact, we must do it for ourselves.

A man heard someone say that he had lost his job and almost lost his family, but fortunately he had found God. The listener replied, "There you were in a corner. God had his knee up on your chest and was breathing in your face and you say *you've* found God?!" God patiently tracks us down and finally confronts us. It's as if we turn away and run from the unconditional love of God; we just can't seem to believe it. But in our heart of hearts we sense that, wherever we run, we cannot escape our own yearning for this unconditional love. All our "escape routes" and diversions eventually disappoint us and our deepest yearnings. We usually come to God by default, as a last resort.

Many people seem to have difficulty understanding and staying in touch with the concept of salvation. In the Christian Scriptures, God finds us; we don't find God. Our action is a *response,* not an instigation.

There is a current and very interesting trend toward rediscovering myths for personal psychological growth. While myths have value as illustrations of human development, they can be used as a way of bypassing the need for salvation. Christian doctrine points out that we do not simply construct our personal myth and "follow our bliss" (as *we* define "bliss"). Rather, the opposite experience seems more frequent: our pain or our addictions force on us an awareness of our need for salvation. Somehow, we seem to want to avoid facing radical insufficiency, the very powerlessness spoken of in Step One of the Twelve Steps. Yet in the kind of recovery process that has a lasting effect, we witness God's action, not ours. Jesus is the primary Christian hero, not us. We must hold on to this important distinction as we recover.

God does come for us, and our reaction may be to ignore God's coming, fight it, try to escape it, or accept and cooperate with it. But whatever we choose, we are the responders. Awareness of how this interaction between God and humans operates is the proper perspective out of which we find satisfaction for our hearts' desires, and the ultimate meaning of life.

NOTE

1. C. G. Jung, Bollingen Series, Vol. IX, *Aion: Researches into the Phenomenology of the Self*, 2d ed. (Princeton: Princeton Univ. Press, 1968).

25

Encountering Ultimate Meaning: The Gospel of John

John's Gospel speaks to the difficulty dealing with losses that comes from the experience of abandonment. In our lack of knowing how to deal with losses in a healthy way, we may try to avoid facing painful losses, seeking to control other people or situations, or to obsess about what is happening, attempting to protect ourselves from experiencing loss. Or we may perceive our losses as crippling and unfair, and our surroundings as too chaotic to control or comprehend, as we sink into depression. But whichever route we take, we often spend time wondering, "what is the meaning of all this?"

We are apt to focus on our own ideas about "how things are or ought to be," and to believe we must solve our own problems. And if we can't, then we believe they will just stay unsolved. This tendency toward self-sufficiency can block our ability to recognize and be open to the saving action of God coming toward us. In times of overwhelming responsibility or depression, we may not realize that one option we have is to ask for help—from other people or from God!

The Gospel of John is good news for those of us who wrestle with these painful difficulties. In this Gospel, we learn that Jesus is God Incarnate, through whom human beings make contact with the presence of God, ultimate reality that never changes. The Gospel shows us how God's presence breaks into our lives through the mystery of Jesus, who came in the flesh as a living, breathing, teaching example that God is real and that a proper relationship with God gives *meaning* to our lives . . . including the painful losses or overwhelming responsibilities. Jesus directly addresses the abandonment issue by promising at the Last Supper that when He leaves, we will not be left alone. God will send the Comforter, the Holy Spirit (John 16). God dwells within us and never abandons us.

John's Gospel reveals the presence of God to us by using at least three approaches: (1) He refers to signs and wonders, (2) he uses expressions involving bold metaphors, and (3) he refers to the temple in Jerusalem in a very special way.

Signs and Wonders

"Signs and wonders" was a phrase used by Hebrews to indicate that God was historically present and active with his people. Jesus makes a direct reference to the "signs and wonders" of the Exodus. In John, Jesus does not perform miracles, he gives the people signs—seven to be exact. Jesus pointed out to the people, perhaps in exasperation, "Unless you people see signs and wonders, you do not believe" (John 4:48). He was calling them to a faith beyond sense perception and personal satisfaction, beyond their self-sufficiency.

One Old Testament example of God's signs and wonders to the Hebrews was putting the rainbow in the heavens as a sign of God's covenant with Noah never to destroy the earth again by water. Another example was circumcision, a sign of the special promise given to Abraham that he would be fruitful. This sign was placed on the very organ of generation, because having many offspring was the way abundance and immortality were expressed in the time of Abraham. After the Exodus under Moses, the most important sign of all was the establishment of the Sabbath as a holy day, a sign of God's presence with the Israelites.

In John's Gospel, the final sign of God's presence comes to the people: Jesus. No longer will God need to give any other kind of sense-perceived sign. Jesus is described in John as the ultimate sign of God's saving action in the world. The Gospel of John emphasizes *God's* saving action in history, not *humanity's* construction of a plan to help the human race self-actualize.

John describes signs of the Kingdom of God in the person of Jesus Christ encountering us in a new context. God's kingdom breaks into our muddled world, bringing us ultimate reality, ultimate meaning.

The signs and wonders offered in John have a distinct purpose: to communicate that God is present, God is here. The first of the signs Jesus worked at Cana in Galilee, turning water into wine. His disciples saw his glory and they believed in him. The term "glory" meant the physical manifestation of the presence of God in the world. When the Bible says the glory of God descended upon the meeting tent of Moses, it meant God was there. And glory is what evokes belief on our part. We believe. We have faith. Faith involves relating to something that we don't control. The opposite of control in relationships is not chaos; the opposite of control is faith. We relate to God coming to meet us.

An evocative image of God coming after us is found in Frances Thompson's "The Hound of Heaven." In his poem, he describes many things he pursued in seeking satisfaction: falling in love, the innocence of children's eyes, and sunrises, sunsets, and other parts of nature. Yet place after place, experience after experience fails to satisfy the deepest yearnings of his heart.

Eventually, the poet finds that nothing but God will satisfy his heart. He finally loses the armor that he has used in the attempt to escape, and comes unprotected to an encounter with this Being that has pursued him. And the Being (God) talks to him, saying,

> All which I took from thee,
>   I did but take not for thy harms
>   but just that thou might'st seek it in my arms.
> All which thy child's mistake fancies as lost,
>   I have stored for thee at home.
>   Rise, clasp my hand and come!

Then the poet realizes that the Being means to bring him satisfaction for these deepest yearnings:

> Halts by me that footfall.
> Is my gloom after all
>   shade of His hand outstretched caressingly?
> "Ah, fondest, blindest, weakest,
>   I am He whom thou seekest.
>   Thou dravest love from thee who dravest me."

Our "child's mistake" (a perfect description of childhood strategies due to neglect, enmeshment, abuse, or abandonment) is that we tried to find meaning in the gifts of God themselves instead of the God of gifts. God pursues us with love; we fear the transformation that this loving encounter will cause in us, perhaps because being changed by contact with someone is unfamiliar, and because change itself involves loss, with which we have difficulty. We have not experienced the kind of contact from which we could learn that we can benefit from change.

Metaphors

Another way Jesus breaks into our reality in a special way is through bold metaphors about the nature of God. The deepest levels of human understanding are the archetypal levels, the spiritual levels. The natural language of the spiritual level of perception is symbol and metaphor. A metaphor is a figure of speech in which a word or phrase is used in place of another to suggest a likeness.[1] Metaphor allows us to connect to something beyond words that is otherwise not understandable.

In John, Jesus uses metaphors to give us a bridge between our reality and the reality in which we directly experience God, and he shows us how God's reality enters our lives so that we are never abandoned.

As in the Exodus, the name used for God in John is "I Am." Jesus helps us with the meaning of God's presence in our lives by declaring God to be like things we know in our environment. He says, "I am . . . " and then gives us a metaphor. When Jesus says, "I am," he identifies himself as God.

> I am the bread of life. He who comes to me will never go hungry, and he who believes in me will never be thirsty. (John 6:35, 48)
> I am the living bread that came down from heaven. (John 6:51)
> I am the light of the world. Whoever follows me will never walk in darkness, but will have the light of life. (John 8:12)
> I am the gate for the sheep. (John 10:7)
> I am the gate; whoever enters through me will be saved. (John 10:9)
> I am the good shepherd. The good shepherd lays down his life for the sheep. (John 10:11) and "I am the good shepherd; I know my sheep and my sheep know me . . . "(John 10:14)
> I am the resurrection and the life. He who believes in me will live, even though he dies. (John 11:25)
> I am the way and the truth and the life. No one comes to the Father except through me. (John 14:6)
> I am the true vine, and my Father is the gardener. (John 15:1) and "I am the vine; you are the branches. If a man remains in me and I in him, he will bear much fruit; apart from me you can do nothing." (John 15:5)

Jesus kept saying, "I came to be with the people who are broken and who need a physician," and who are aware that he was that physician (Matt. 9:12). He dealt with people who had lost all of the defenses that they could put between themselves and the unconditional love that God gave them. It is precisely in our meaninglessness, in our brokenness, that we meet Jesus.

This paradoxical concept is being revived by the Twelve-Step programs. There is something that we must encounter in our humanity that is a corrective, or healing, experience, and it involves shared brokenness in a group. The realization that we are loved in our most shameful aspects, in our brokenness, undoes shame, provides a new, solid basis for self-esteem, and gives a new, freer, more truthful way of relating to people. Jesus heals our brokenness from the experience of abandonment: difficulty facing loss, excessive self-sufficiency, tendency to control, and lack of a sense of meaning.

The Temple

God's presence in our lives is particularly illustrated through the image of the temple, used repeatedly in the Gospel of John. In classical times, there was a difference between a temple and a church or synagogue. A church or synagogue was the assembly place for people to pray to God. A temple, however, was God's residence, the place where humanity came into direct contact with the deity. Sacrifice was offered *in front* of the temple, not *in* the temple, because that was God's home.

The temple in Jerusalem was a place where a person literally encountered God. The Old Testament Jews had tremendous pride and faith that because God's temple was in Jerusalem, they would never be destroyed. When the Jews finally were overrun it must have shattered their particular understanding of God's special presence and protection for Jerusalem with all its historical precedent.

In John's Gospel, Jesus said, "Destroy this temple and in three days I will raise it up" (John 2:19). John adds, "Actually, he was talking about the temple of his body" (John 3:21), implying that the person of Jesus Christ *is* the temple, the literal dwelling place of the deity.

In John's Gospel, when Jesus died on the cross, the Jewish temple curtain covering the holiest of places was torn in two. The temple as a tangible building was no longer relevant. There was no longer a building that contains the Holy of Holies. The new temple is now in the person of Jesus Christ, and by extension it is also the body of Christ, the members of Christ's church.

Some years after the crucifixion, Paul said, "You must know that your body is a temple of the Holy Spirit who is within—the Spirit you have received from God" (1 Cor. 6:19). That is, we now come into the presence of God on earth through our humanity and in our human relationships. Jesus had forever changed how we contact God: the temple of God, the contact point with God on earth, is in our humanity, particularly in the scandalous areas of our brokenness where Jesus Christ chooses to encounter us.

We still have not absorbed the import of this concept or we wouldn't wantonly kill other human beings or do the destructive and humiliating things to other human beings that we do. All people are temples of God, dwelling places of the deity through Jesus Christ.

At times we may have trouble realizing the presence of God within us and wonder, "Where are you, God?" We don't *feel* we are the dwelling places of God. We don't *see* God's action in our lives very easily. We seem to lose the meaning in our lives, and this leads to a desolate feeling of abandonment. Actually, God does not abandon us; perhaps our *ideas* of God become inadequate. When our outmoded ideas of God collapse, we feel that God has "gone away." Actually, only our ideas have "gone away," and we are faced with the mysterious presence of a Higher Power for whom we have no name.

This can be especially painful when we believe we have been faithfully following God's will in our lives, and then disaster strikes. Not only do we suffer the disaster, but our predictable, "safe" relationship with God seems demolished as well.

Our Deepest Need Answered

Our deep yearning for meaning and perspective is answered by John's Gospel, which presents a picture of God in the active role and us in the responsive role of the relationship between God and human beings. John's Gospel addresses the pain of having experienced childhood abandonment directly, revealing the meaning of a relationship with God in our lives, and giving us the promise that God will not abandon us.

NOTE

1. *Webster's New Collegiate Dictionary.*

26

Amazing Stories: Our Lives from God's Perspective

The Scriptures in John's Gospel that illustrate God's promise to meet our yearning for ultimate meaning and perspective are not parables, but living stories of Jesus' interaction with people, especially Simon Peter. Since Peter was a fisherman by profession, these stories also involve water. Stories that involve Peter, Jesus, and water give us great lessons about our unconscious. By looking at Scripture allegorically, these stories become descriptions of our soul's deepest experience. They illustrate how our lives are dealt with from God's perspective as God puts us properly in touch with reality, or *ultimate meaning.*

Our relationship to water is parallel to our relationship to our unconscious mind and the things that dwell there. Our bodies are made up mostly of water. We are born out of water—the amniotic fluid in the womb is like seawater. And yet, we are not water creatures. We need to have water by the cupful to live or we will die. But if we are completely underwater for too long, we will also die. In the same way, our minds are mostly unconscious—many scientists estimate that the conscious part of our mind is much smaller than the unconscious part. We must have contact with the unconscious mind through dreaming ("by the cupful"), or we will compensate by hallucinating during the day.

We are fascinated with what lives beneath the actual water, and we catch various sea creatures for food and sustenance. Old creatures that have changed very little over the centuries swim down there like archetypal realities in the unconscious. In the gospel stories, these "fish" resemble dream elements that slip through our fingers. When we can catch dream elements and bring them to our conscious minds, the meaning we find there is also sustaining to our spiritual growth. So our relationship to water and the life beneath it is very much like our relationship to this realm we call the unconscious mind.

We are given many lessons in the Bible about our relationship to water and therefore to our unconscious mind. Let's look at several of them that involve Peter, who represents our conscious ego. Three of the stories we have selected are from Matthew or Luke, while one is from John. As we shall see, the ultimate meaning of Peter's relationship with Jesus seems to be revealed to us in the final encounter betrween the two, before Jesus' ascension, described in John.

Peter Casting Out His Nets (Luke 5:1–10)

One of the earliest experiences Simon Peter had with Jesus was after he and his shipmates had spent a long night fishing and caught nothing. The story in which Peter spent a long night catching nothing reminds us of an experience called "the dark night of the soul," when we feel so alone and cut off from God.

The next day Jesus got into Peter's boat and told him to put the boat out a little way from shore so Jesus could teach the crowd. The little boat can represent the thin hull of our ego defenses on top of the water, our own unconscious depths. And then . . .

> when he had finished speaking he said to Simon, "Put out into deep water, and lower your nets for a catch."

Jesus promises that when he asks us to lower the nets of our conscious categories, our mind, we will catch something.

> Simon answered, "Master, we have been hard at it all night long and have caught nothing. But if you say so, I will lower the nets." Upon doing this they caught such a great number of fish that their nets were at the breaking point.

When we are young, encountering the experience of Jesus often "breaks our mind" in a way. Seeing teenagers coming home from a spiritual retreat gives some idea of how shattered, in a good sense, they are. It "blows their mind," they say.

Peter, not being a stupid person, falls on his knees and says,

> "Leave me, Lord. I am a sinful man." For indeed, amazement at the catch they had made seized him and all his shipmates.
>
> Jesus said to Simon, "Do not be afraid. From now on you will be catching men."

The message Jesus has for Simon is, "All that you have learned about searching for life in the depths of the sea, I will teach you to do with the depths of human beings." And so, Simon went to shore, left his nets and his boats, and followed Jesus.

Jesus Calms the Sea (Matt. 8:23–27 and Luke 8:22–25)

This story is one in which the disciples and Jesus were out on a lake in the boat, and without warning a storm came up. The storm on the lake can represent our lives when chaos is going on all around us. When we are in a boat in a storm, we are truly out of control. There are a few things a good sailor knows to do, but beyond these we are at the mercy of the water and the seaworthiness of the boat itself.

Psychologically speaking, the opposite of control is not chaos, but faith. We need faith when we have to continue to relate to something we no longer control. This story is an excellent example of what a proper attitude of faith is.

Peter, Jesus, and the others are in the boat, being tossed about by the storm. They turn to Jesus, who is asleep in the back of the boat, and say, "Lord, we are perishing." Or, to put it in our language, "We are going down! Doesn't it matter to you?"

And Jesus wakes up and looks at them. He doesn't say, "Pass the bucket and put on your life jackets!" He says, "Where is your faith?" And then *he* stands up and rebukes the wind and the sea, and they became calm.

When the sea is calm, the disciples say, "What manner of man is this that even the wind and the sea obey him?" Wind and sea are old mythological symbols for the primal forces of nature that can either give life or destroy. The wind is a masculine symbol; the seawater is feminine. Just as Jesus is master of the external elements of nature, he is master of the internal elements of nature in the unconscious mind, both masculine and feminine (and men and women have both elements). It is our relationship to Jesus that ultimately calms wind and sea. That seems to be the lesson, because in the story the apostles come to land almost immediately after this.

Peter Walks on Water (Matt. 14:28–33)

This next story begins after Jesus has fed people bread and fish: bread from the land, fish from the sea—conscious and unconscious. The disciples set out on a night sea journey, similar to the mythic "hero's night sea journey." At about two in the morning, the boat is making no headway in the water because the wind is blowing against it. And then the disciples see Jesus coming toward them, walking on water.

HEALING FROM ABANDONMENT 179

Now, human beings can't walk on water, except perhaps on a lake in the winter! If you look at this story symbolically, the message could be that our conscious minds can't deal directly with the unconscious part. If we do try, we may "go down" into hallucinations or delusions. We can't seem to function in such a dream world; we have to exist within our own fragile arena that we call consciousness. In this story, however, seen allegorically, Jesus is capable of walking directly on the surface of the unconscious.

And the disciples cry out in fear, "It's a ghost!"

Then Peter says, "Master, if it is really you, bid me come to you over the water."

And Jesus says, "Come, Peter." Come on out, directly into the unconscious mind. Look at all this unconscious material in your life. And Peter gets out of the boat and starts walking on the water. As he is walking, he begins to notice the violence of the wind and the waves, and down he goes! He sinks. And Jesus is right there. He grabs Peter and says, "Peter, where is your faith?" The rule might be stated, "When you venture out into your unconscious mind, don't keep your eyes only on the violent forces around you. Keep your eyes on me." Jesus then helps Peter, sputtering, back into the boat.

The lesson for us in this story is that when we delve into the material in our unconscious mind, during the process, we need to keep our eyes on Christ, not just on the harmful, painful, dysfunctional things that have happened to us, and all of the frightening changes that may occur in our lives. It is such a temptation to think that when we look at the wind and the water all around us, the memories and the enormous feelings from our past, we must *focus* on these things. We can even get caught up in habitually focusing on all the miserable things we humans do to each other and our environment. Tune in to a news broadcast; look at all the bad news, the wars, the crimes, the storms, the problems. These can quickly lead us to despair and a sense of meaninglessness. As we go back through our childhood memories and see the painful, abusive events we survived, we may sink unless we have some way to make some sense out of it, to see its meaning from a perspective of recovery. In the recovery process, a Christian is asked by Christ to "keep your eyes on me."

This doesn't mean we focus just on Christ and avoid examining these disturbing, painful things. We do not recover by ignoring, denying, or distorting them; we reexperience them as we look at them. But if they become *objects of continuing preoccupation,* down we go.

Sometimes people need a positive antidote to all the painful memories they must review in the process of recovery. The recovery process itself can become an object of preoccupation. People can get very practiced at therapy, and they begin to think, "Looking at all the painful, dark, horrible parts of my past and present makes me realistic. Life is grim and real." At such times, it is very important to say, "Wait a minute! There is grace. Learn how to accentuate the positive and look at your resources." The ultimate reality is that in relationship to Christ we can dare to deal with these dark parts of ourselves, trusting in faith that we will break through the barriers they have created and enter into the experience of a full life in recovery. One of the striking things about Twelve-Step meetings is the laughter—in the midst of the revelations of dysfunctional behaviors and painful secrets—as people learn to focus on the joy and security of a relationship to God.

Jesus Appears to Peter After the Resurrection (John 21:1–14)

The final story of Peter and water offers insights about how our capacity to deal with the material in our unconscious can be strengthened. The scene takes place after Peter's denial of Christ, and after he has seen the resurrected Jesus, but he is still struggling with the pain and disappointment of having failed to keep his promise not to deny Jesus. Finally, perhaps remembering that he had first met Jesus while fishing, he tells his friends,

> "I am going out to fish."
> "We will join you," they replied, and went off to get into their boat. All through the night they caught nothing.

Here is another image of the disciples' experience of the dark night of the soul, only this time they are wrestling with their feelings and thoughts about Jesus' death and resurrection. Once again, Jesus encounters Peter after a long night of fishing and catching nothing and asks Peter to cast out his nets and make a catch of fish.

> Just after daybreak Jesus was standing on the shore, though none of the disciples knew it was Jesus.
> He said to them, "Children, have you caught anything to eat?"
> "Not a thing," they answered.
> "Cast your net off to the starboard side," he suggested, "and you will find something." So they made a cast, and took so many fish they could not haul the net in.
> Then the disciple Jesus loved cried out to Peter, "It is the Lord!" On hearing it was the Lord, Simon Peter threw on some clothes—he was stripped—and jumped into the water.

Poor Peter was totally stripped by this time. The truth of his cowardice and frailty has been shown to him in a stark way. We are stripped of everything we have that is between us and the mercy of God at such times in our lives: our pride, our posturings, our self-reliance.

Peter leapt into the water and went toward shore. When we recognize Christ's presence, we need not hesitate to plunge into our unconscious minds and head for understanding and release! This resembles Peter's previous experience of walking on the water, and it is also an image of baptism.

> Meanwhile the other disciples came in the boat, towing the net full of fish. Actually they were not far from land—no more than a hundred yards.
> When they had landed, they saw a charcoal fire there with a fish laid on it and some bread.
> "Bring some of the fish you just caught," Jesus told them.

Note the emphasis on who caught the fish: the fish that *you* caught. In other words, throughout our lives we will encounter these realities from our unconscious depths, but now *through the power of the resurrection* of Jesus we will know how to deal with them and assimilate them.

> Simon Peter went aboard and hauled ashore the net loaded with sizable fish—one hundred fifty-three of them! In spite of the great number, the net was not torn.

That the nets did not tear is an important point. Compare this to the earlier story in which the nets did tear. Now, by the power of the resurrection, the "nets" of Peter's conscious understanding can hold the life surging up from his depths. And so can ours.

The Sower and the Seed

Once more in examining recovery, we look at this rich parable of a farmer planting seed. The fourth soil condition Jesus described is that of fertile ground.

> And, finally, some seed fell on fertile ground—on good soil. It went in deep and then it sprang up and yielded an abundant harvest, 30, 60 and 100 fold.

Fertile ground yields up a good harvest only if it is well tended. We have to farm, be there every day, aerating the soil, watering, and making sure there's enough light for the plants. We must go through the passage of seasons, and show extraordinary attentiveness to be a farmer.

The point here is diligence and patience: the diligence of a farmer, the patience needed to wait for plants to mature. We find that growth in recovery does not occur at the speed of light, or of a jet plane, or even of a thought. We grow at the speed of plant growth, the agricultural tempo. The soil of our lives, in our recovery from abandonment, needs to be tended almost the way fertile soil requires tending on a daily basis. As the weather and the seasons change, and the plant itself goes through transformation, we must not abandon our task.

The temptation of those of us who have experienced childhood abandonment is to lose touch with meaning and perspective in our lives. Having had little or no ongoing care-giving structure to lean on in childhood, we may be all too familiar with the void created by lack of parental presence. We can float around in it for days, weeks, and months and not be aware that we are experiencing this void at all. Creating and living within our own life structure by which we take care of our physical, emotional, intellectual, and psychological needs, and perhaps most especially our *spiritual needs,* seems to be almost too much trouble. We may enter recovery with great relief and hope, then after a while, find that we are no longer in a state of alarm or great pain, and so the recovery exercises don't seem meaningful. We who are used to operating only in extremes begin to wander away from the daily routine of tending the soil of our lives.

But as we heal from the effects of abandonment, we establish the habits of recovery and can gradually overcome the problem of the changing conditions in our lives. Now we're dealing with the problems of maintaining the life that has been generated through our conversion and the beginning of our recovery, to harvest the bounty God has for us in our lives.

27

Redirecting Our Deep Longing for Perfect Meaning and Perspective to God

The three sets of guidelines we have used to find recovery from neglect, enmeshment, and abuse are also applicable to our recovery from abandonment. These include the last three steps of the Twelve Steps, meditations and journaling from the Scriptures, and psychospiritual exercises. These exercises are based on recording our dreams and on journaling as ways to explore deeper levels of our unconscious minds. As we grow more and more adept at dealing with necessary losses and change, we are able to move more fully into the life for which we were meant.

The Twelve Steps: Steps Ten, Eleven, and Twelve[1]

Step Ten is, "Continued to take personal inventory and when we were wrong promptly admitted it."

Step Eleven is, "Sought through prayer and meditation to improve our conscious contact with God as we understood God, praying only for the knowledge of God's will for us and the power to carry that out." We not only examine ourselves, but we also try to stay in conscious contact with God.

Step Twelve is, "Having had a spiritual awakening as the result of these steps, we tried to carry the message to other persons and to practice these principles in all our affairs."

Steps Ten through Twelve help us mature the process of developing a relationship with a nonabandoning Being—God, the Indwelling Trinity. These steps, sometimes called the maintenance steps, are spiritual tools that point us toward finding the meaning and purpose in our lives. This provides us with the experience of the Indwelling Trinity. If the Trinity is within us, then we are not abandoned, but forever in contact with an ultimate reality that gives our lives meaning. The psychospiritual exercises described later provide a way to connect to Steps Ten and Eleven. The dream-recording section can be related to a prayer and meditation process in Step Eleven, and the brief journaling exercise can be a form of Step Ten.

Lessons from the Scriptures

STORIES OF JESUS, PETER, AND WATER

Review the comments in chapter 26 about how the stories of Jesus, Peter, and water can teach us about our unconscious. Apply this concept to your own life by responding in your journal to the following questions.

1. What situations in your life seem to be out of your control, the way Peter and the other disciples were out of control in the storm on the sea?

2. Take one of the situations you listed above, and meditate for a few minutes. Picture yourself on the boat with Peter, waking up Jesus and explaining the situation in your life. Then watch to see how Jesus responds. Write a description of what you learn from this meditation.

3. Repeat this exercise for each of the situations you listed above.

THE SOWER AND THE SEED

1. List in your journal the "habits of recovery" you have recognized that you need in order to tend to the spiritual soil of your life.

2. It is possible to be in denial about the things that have *improved* in our lives once we are no longer in a state of alarm and pain. List in your journal any areas of your life that used to create alarm or pain for you that have improved.

3. List any changes in your life that are ahead for you. They could include major changes such as moving, changing jobs, getting married, having a child, or medium-sized changes such as a change in the place or time of a meeting, the time you go to bed or get up, what you eat, or adding something new to your schedule such as a daily quiet time or attending a class.

4. Write in your own words a recovery-oriented statement about your willingness to rely on God's grace and power to empower you to make these changes. For example: "I will overcome my

resistance to change by relying on your strength each day, each hour, O Lord."

5. Use the statement you have written as a prayer whenever you feel the sense of meaninglessness coming up, or when the effort to make the change seems to be too much.

Psychospiritual Exercises

Spiritual recovery in this area involves looking at our whole life and being able to go through transitions and the growth process of change and conversion without letting the fear of annihilation stop us. In doing this, we come into contact with our unconscious mind, the deeper part of our life. This process is not so much like the surgery process in healing of memories, but more like taking our spiritual pulse, sensing more about the growth patterns of the deeper levels of the psyche.

Two methods, dream recording and journaling, are ways of monitoring the unconscious mind. The images in our dreams act like an early warning system from our unconscious mind, offering us a constructive commentary and interpretation of our conscious experience.

DREAM RECORDING

Recording dreams is a way of connecting to a greater reality that comes to us through the symbols of our unconscious mind. At times we may approach problems or painful situations with strategies that seem to be stuck in a rut. No new options occur to us. In our "stuckness," we may be facing our difficulty of dealing with necessary losses involved in change that comes from childhood experiences of abandonment.

In facing life's changes, we might think of slight adjustments on one or two specific and familiar strategies that worked for us in the past, but eventually we may find that even these variations don't work. Then we feel really stuck, unable to break out and find new approaches to our situation.

However, if we pay attention to our dreams we often find that our dreams compensate for the unproductive, single-minded solutions in our conscious minds, and give us symbolic messages that broaden our thinking. It isn't that the problem goes away, but we see it in a greater context and we are able to break out and develop a new way of approaching the problem.

After experiencing childhood abandonment, we often have a sense of the absurdity of our daily existence, as though our lives don't mean anything. Recording and evaluating our dreams can give us a connection to deeper patterns in ourselves and restore a sense of meaning to our lives.

There is a strong religious tradition of respecting dreams. A nightmare is seen as God tapping us on the shoulder and saying we need to wake up and pay attention to our lives. A recurring dream is seen as saying we haven't attended to the dream yet, so it keeps coming back. There are enough examples of this in the Christian tradition to say that dream recording can be an integral part of the Eleventh Step, "making conscious contact with God."

The blessing, or Spirit of God, was often given to the dreamers in the Bible. Joseph (of the Old Testament) was referred to as a dreamer by his brothers, yet he was the one who was in touch with God. Although he was sold off to Egypt, he found that through dream interpretation he could bring even the Pharaoh into contact with God's plan. (The New Testament Joseph might also be known as Joseph the Dreamer. He received word in a dream not to fear to take Mary as his wife. Later he was given the warning from an angel in a dream to flee to Egypt. Still later, he received word in a dream to come back from Egypt. He follows these dreams.)

One of the biblical patriarchs had a remarkable dream experience that solved a most difficult problem. As a young man, Jacob had tricked his older brother Esau out of a birthright. Jacob then fled Esau's anger and spent many years away, learning the hard lessons of maturity. But finally, Jacob realized that he had to return to his home—and he knew Esau would be waiting for him. Jacob sent gifts ahead to Esau to placate him, but then realized he had no legitimate excuse to shield himself from Esau's anger. The day before the confrontation, Jacob sent everyone else ahead and spent the night alone. He was at an impasse.

That night, Jacob encountered a mysterious being; he wrestled with his own shadow, or deepest fear, almost like a figure in a dream. The struggle went on for hours. Just as light was coming, and he was about to overcome the opponent in the dream, the figure touched his hip and wounded him.

> Then the man said, "Let me go, for it is daybreak."
> But Jacob said, "I will not let you go until you bless me."
> "What is your name?" the man asked.
> He answered, "Jacob."
> Then the man said, "You shall no longer be spoken of as Jacob, but as Israel, because you have contended with divine and human beings and have prevailed." (Gen. 32:27–29)

Jacob wrestled with the dream, and tried to get its meaning and was wounded by it. Woundedness *was* the solution Jacob needed but could not obtain consciously. Jacob, now Israel, limped off to meet Esau, who, in seeing his hobbled brother, forgot all his anger and tearfully embraced him. The dream helped Israel find a relationship *in his brokenness,* the paradoxical solution that leads to reconciliation.[2]

In Step Eleven, it is important that we remain open to God on a daily basis through our dreams. Dreams have been rediscovered as messengers of God by writers such as Robert Johnson, Morton Kelsey, and John Sanford. Our dreams are important for us to pay attention to and to honor. A rabbi once said that a dream unexamined is like a letter from God that is left unopened.

What to Do

When we are experiencing distress or making decisions, or we don't know where to turn, it is helpful to listen for God's will through every avenue possible. One important avenue is dreams, so during such times we need to start recording our dreams. Here is a simple method of looking at dreams, adapted from Robert Johnson's method in the book *Inner Work.*[3]

1. Recording the Dream: Put a notebook and pencil by your bed. When you wake up from a dream, turn on the light and write it down. You may need to go in the bathroom, or tape a pencil to a penlight so as not to disturb anyone else's sleep. Do your best to write down as much as you can remember.

2. Associations: Either immediately after recording the dream or some time later, reread your description of the dream. Certain elements of the dream will stand out from the rest, or will seem to have a certain impact on you. For example, you might have written, "There I am and I see a blue dog." Blue? Click! The word *blue* just strikes you as unusual. It seems to have a psychic significance. Circle that element and keep reading.

When you have circled about three or four elements, move to a clean space after your dream account and, one at a time, put each circled word in the middle of a blank page. Draw lines out from the circle like spokes from the hub of a wheel. Start making associations to the dream element, whatever comes to mind. Avoid making associations to the associations themselves—stick to the original word or phrase from the dream.

Go all the way around the wheel, writing as many associations as you can think of dealing with the word in the circle. As you associate these things, you start "unpacking" this symbol from your unconscious and getting closer to its meaning.

Repeat the association process for each dream element you noted. Among these associations, note the ones that seem to stand out as significant.

Example

Assemble these into a separate list after the space where you worked on the associations.

3. Application: Apply the dream account and the significant associations to your present life situation. What is the dream telling you about your life today? What action seems to be indicated for you to take? Spend some time with these questions to see what answers occur to you.

4. Action: Obey the dream. Do one or more of the actions you described in the previous step to carry out the apparent directive of the dream. The action can be either direct or as a ritual, which is a good way to respond to a symbol.

For example, a man kept dreaming he was being poisoned. By working on the associations, he realized he was eating junk food all the time. So he bought the greasiest hamburger he could find and buried it in the backyard with full honors. It was a perfect ritual to signify his obedience to the message to put healthy food into his body instead of junk food.

KEEPING A SPIRITUAL JOURNAL

Keeping a brief spiritual journal is a way of contacting the unconscious. It can be a useful tool for working Step Ten as well—continuing to take inventory and, when we are wrong, promptly admitting it. People have found that this brief journaling exercise is also a good way to center and relax, to let go of worries and conflicts.

Many of us are extroverts for whom it is difficult to sit down and keep a deeply detailed journal. We may have wished for a meaningful journal process for busy people. A brief form of journaling, developed by Father Ray Roh, O.S.B. at Pecos Benedictine Monastery in Pecos, New Mexico, offers just that.[4]

Journaling guides us to the center of ourselves and gets us in touch with these deeper areas where God touches us, if we're willing to open up to them. We record the blessings and the difficulties of the day, and what we experienced by getting in contact with our inner selves and then more deeply with God. By doing this brief process daily, over time we can construct a record about God's subtle influences in our lives. By reviewing different periods in our lives, we may begin to see a pattern—some deeper threads, or the bigger picture—and we can begin to develop better understanding of our life context and its meaning.

We begin to see that God was working all the time, and that the times we thought we were trudging along alone, we were actually being carried. As illustrated by the single set of footprints in the sand described in the poem "Footsteps," a journal can help us know the answer to the question, "Where were you, God?" Thus, journaling also reduces our sense of abandonment and helps us develop an ongoing relationship with God.

What to Do

1. Begin by writing a *short* statement in your journal about how you feel at this time. Use just a few words to describe your interior state, both physically and emotionally, that is, I'm tired, I'm happy, I'm sad, my neck aches. Practicing this step helps you learn how to settle down and get in touch with your inner self, a process called centering.

2. Draw a line down the middle of a clean page and put a minus sign above the left side and a plus sign above the right side, like a ledger with debits and credits. List all the debits or shortcomings under the minus side, things that you have done or failed to do, or negative experiences that have happened during the day. Then, under the plus side, list the positive things that you have done, or strengths that have come forth during the day. This is rather like counting your blessings. Keep listing the blessings until you get at least one more on the plus side of the page than you have under the minus side.

A difficulty for many of us is that we can make a "searching and fearless moral inventory" of ourselves, but many of our shortcomings aren't that blatant. We haven't beaten people up or totaled a car or lost a lot of money. Our problem is more often related to developing ego strength. So the challenge for us may be to make an inventory of our strengths as well as our faults.

3. To get in touch with yourself further, say your name like a mantra, a centering prayer. Say it ten times, in a slow and loving way, followed by quietly listening to anything your Self may tell or show you. It is helpful to write down or draw a picture of these messages from the Self.

4. After recording any messages you received from your Self, say the name you use for God or to address your Higher Power (Father, Jesus, Lord, Teacher, and so forth) in the same intimate, slow, loving way, ten times. After this, listen to any messages or pictures that God may give you, and record them.

5. After these four steps, close the journal and kiss the day either hello, or goodbye (depending on whether you do the exercise in the morning or at night).

A Method for Step Eleven

Another structured way to do Step Eleven is called the *Lectio Divina,* a four-step Benedictine prayer form. It has been around for about fifteen hundred years and is a wonderful way to pray from the Scriptures.

1. Read a Scripture.
2. Reflect on the Scripture (meditation).
3. Pray out of the reflections.
4. Contemplate a while, listening for God's message to you.

Remember to make a note of any messages you receive, as you did in the previous exercise.

NOTES

1. See Appendix A for all twelve Steps as developed by Alcoholics Anonymous.
2. John Sanford, *The Man Who Wrestled With God* (New York: Paulist Press, 1987).
3. Robert Johnson, *Inner Work* (San Francisco: Harper & Row, 1986).
4. Adapted from Fr. Ray Roh, O.S.B., *Keeping a Spiritual Journal,* Pamphlet No. 80 (Pecos: Dove Publications, 1978).

Conclusion: A Life in Recovery

Ever since God placed Adam and Eve in the Garden of Eden, God has sought to be in a life-giving, loving relationship with us. Whenever anything comes between us and God, God offers the remedy, the antidote, the solution. But there is a problem that keeps us from looking to God for the help we need.

We human beings are flawed. There is a missing element that prevents our experiencing ourselves as whole. This missing element has been called original sin, and it has been passed down through generations by dysfunctional family experiences. We have fled from the pain of it and from the God who offers to heal us. We might even flee into addictions and codependence, and in the process even the very healing, life-giving *desire* for God may become distorted.

By examining the evidence of God's healing action for ourselves, we can begin to recapture, or perhaps grasp for the first time, the exciting news that Christian faith has much to offer those who seek wholeness—perhaps the vital link to completing the picture of recovery.

Christian conversion says there are two necessary actions for entering recovery. First, we must somehow stop turning to our addictions as the objects of the skewed, misdirected deep energies of our being. Second, we must be *open to God's coming toward us,* just as our first task as infants was to be open to care and nurture from our care givers.

The Message Comes Repeatedly from Scripture

God, taking the initiative, lovingly reaches out to us and intervenes in our lives. God sends messengers as God did to Joseph in the New Testament, Jacob and Joseph in the Old Testament. God runs toward us, forgiving us and taking care of us as the father took care of his younger son in the parable of the Prodigal Son. God touches us to heal us in our shadow side, in the very places where we are broken and ashamed, as the Good Samaritan tended the wounded man.

God's desire is to make us whole, to give us the gift of relationship to others. God opens our eyes to spiritual reality as God did to the man born blind (see

John 9), and to choice and to the joy and energizing power of sacrifice. God opens our eyes to our absolute *need for God* in the stories of Peter, as God healed Peter by breaking him open to his weakness and then to new life, like gently breaking an egg. And God calls us into the mystery of God through our encounter with Jesus Christ in the Gospel of John. The central point of contact with God on earth is Jesus Christ, who identified himself with broken humanity, came to be in our midst, and showed us that, like him, we are the temple of God, God's home on earth.

Spiritual Recovery Leads to Changed Attitudes

A change in some of our fundamental attitudes toward life becomes evident when we begin to redirect our unmet needs toward God.

1. *Willingness to Respond to Yearnings by Seeking God:* We begin to identify the unmet longings that are involved in the circumstances and events of our daily lives. Even though these are painful, we are more able to deal with the event and less likely to medicate the pain with substances, behaviors, or accomplishments. Whenever an unmet longing comes up, we turn to God and we are more likely to include joy and hope in our response, because these occasions offer us the opportunity to discover how we can move closer to God as fulfillment for our longings.

For example, when we feel the painful symptoms of our neglect issues, such as emotional numbness (unconsciousness) or disappointment with someone who seems to have let us down, we know that this involves our deep yearning for perfect care giving, and we are reminded to seek God the Parent as the answer to this yearning. We can then start dealing with neglect in a Twelve-Step program or in religious participation. We are less likely to turn the care of our inner child over to other people. We begin to stop relating in ways which we, in effect, neglect ourselves, thereby participating in creating our own painful state of deprivation.

When our enmeshment issues appear and we notice the faults of others, we are willing to look at the possibility that we are projecting our shadow side onto the person we resent. We can use these observations to learn about ourselves and deal with our projection and enmeshment by refurbishing our boundary system through the projection-withdrawal process, Twelve-Step meetings, or by prayerful meditation. We call on Jesus Christ to fill our deepest yearnings for loving human companionship. We clarify the distinction between ourselves and others and resist setting ourselves up for dysfunctional relationships in which we view others as extensions of ourselves, or view ourselves as an extension of someone else.

When our abuse issues arise, we may notice that we are being overcompliant with someone in authority, or we are being rebellious and chaotic with those we love. At such times we can know that these behaviors may be coming from our deep yearning for power and freedom. As we begin addressing our own abuse issues, informed through a connection with God, the Holy Spirit, we can begin to modify or let go of relationships in which we allow ourselves to be abused by someone, or in which we ourselves are the abuser.

When, because of our abandonment issues, we feel we cannot cope with a loss or change in our lives, or are unable to figure out what is going on, we can know that we are yearning for connection to ultimate meaning through God, the Holy Trinity. We can then start directing this yearning toward the Holy Trinity dwelling within us. By recording our dreams and practicing spiritual journaling, we can open up new approaches to dealing with loss or change, informed by God through our unconscious minds. In this way, we can maintain our recovery through life's changes by focusing on our relationship to the unchanging Trinity, which becomes the central meaning in our lives.

2. *Increased Ability to Act Properly in the World:* The more we are in touch with God, the more we are able to use our power properly as Jesus illustrated in Mark's Gospel: laying down his life for us, healing brokenness, and fighting evil.

Laying Down Our Lives for Others: Our recovery and increased connection to God enables us to maintain a well of living water from which to draw to give to others. We intuitively know better how to love our neighbor as ourselves, because of our growing love and respect for ourselves as temples of God. We have increased awareness of ourselves as God's beloved creations who have meaning and purpose. Little by little, we can let go of our need to make *our solutions* work for others. We can show up, do our part, and rely on God to complete God's purpose for other people. The Twelfth Step points out that when we have had the kind of spiritual awakening we are describing we will try to carry this message to others. And the wisdom of the program says that doing this is the best way to keep the fruits of the spirit (that we are discovering) alive!

Healing Brokenness: We can do our part to heal brokenness in the world by making amends when our actions have harmed others. We become people characterized by the ability to forgive. We allow ourselves to process the full range of emotions necessary to reach complete and lasting forgiveness, pushing through denial, pushing through anger, dealing with bargaining, going through depression, coming to acceptance.

Childhood Developmental Stage[1]	Contact Point (Archetype) Activated[2]	Predominant Learning Style	Family-of-Origin Experience[3]	Dysfunctional Survival Trait[4]	Drug Effect Desired[5]	Twelve Steps	Gospels	Experience of God	Psychospiritual Exercises
1. Trust vs Mistrust	Yearning for Perfect Parenting	Classical Conditioning[6]	Neglect	Too Dependent or Antidependent or Needless/Wantless	Sedative	One Two Three	Matthew	Father (Parent) Structure (Masc.) Nurture (Fem.) Nurturing Provider	Life Affirmation Baseline, Success Experience Baseline
2. Autonomy vs Shame and Doubt	Yearning for Perfect Companionship and Personal Development	Social Learning[7]	Enmeshment	Too Vulnerable or Invulnerable	Euphoriant	Four Five Six	Luke	Son (Child) Companion on Life's Journey	Projection Withdrawal
3. Initiative vs Guilt	Yearning for Perfect Power and Freedom	Operant Conditioning[8]	Abuse	Good/Perfect or Bad/Rebellious	Stimulant	Seven Eight Nine	Mark	Holy Spirit (Evident in Gifts, Works) Acting in Our Lives	Healing of Memories[9]
4. Industry vs Inferiority	Yearning for Perfect Meaning and Perspective	Cognitive Modeling[10,11]	Abandonment	Overmature (Controlling) or Extremely Immature (Chaotic)	Hallucinogenic	Ten Eleven Twelve	John	Indwelling Trinity, Our Lives from God's Perspective	Dream Recording[12] Brief Spiritual Journaling[13]

Figure 6: How Christian Spirituality Pulls Together the Twelve Steps and Depth Psychology

Fighting Evil: Truth is more accessible as our denial and delusion crumble away. When our compulsions and addictions are in remission, one day at a time, we can be more wholly present to contact God and more resistant to that which would destroy life rather than give it. This attitude can permeate our lives individually, as a nation, and as dwellers on the planet Earth.

The Spiritual Aspect of Our Brokenness and the Spiritual Recovery Tools

The chart in Figure 6 gives an overview of the spiritual recovery path described in this book. It summarizes how Christian spirituality pulls together the spiritual recovery path outlined in the Twelve Steps with the healing offered by the tools of depth psychology. The links between recovery and psychological/spiritual healing methods illustrate the marvelous integration of heart, mind, soul, and body that is possible with a healthy and vital Christian faith.

No longer need we fear a harsh, intimidating, punitive God who demands perfection and promises dire punishment for our faults and mistakes. No longer need we despair over a distant God, busily engaged in more important business than ours. No longer need we try to manipulate God as an extension of ourselves, to carry out our wishes and do our will.

Meeting each other in truth, sharing our brokenness, turning to God for satisfaction of our deepest longings, we can be strengthened in our journey toward psychological and spiritual wholeness. As we do, we develop within us a well-nourished central core out of which we move into relationships marked by our sharing with others the God-given reality and fulfillment we have found.

What might happen to those who take this journey we are describing we do not know, but we think Dietrich Bonhoeffer, the German martyr, came close to the answer when he said: "If we answer the call to discipleship, where will it lead us? What decision and partings will be demanded? To answer this question we should have to go to Him, for only He knows the answer; only Jesus Christ, who bids us follow Him, knows the journey's end. But we do know that it will be a road of boundless mercy. Discipleship means joy."[14] And that has been our experience, too.

NOTES

1. Erik Erikson, *Childhood and Society* (New York: W.W. Norton, 1963).
2. Anthony Stevens, *Archetypes* (New York: Quill, 1983).
3. John Bradshaw, "Bradshaw on the Family," PBS Telecast, 1987.

4. Pia Mellody, with Andrea Wells Miller and J. Keith Miller, *Facing Codependence* (San Francisco: Harper San Francisco, 1989).

5. Carol Roberts, "The Wounded Feeling Function and Dependency Behaviors," Presentation at Journey into Wholeness Conference, Hendersonville, NC, Nov. 9–13, 1987.

6. J. B. Watson and R. Rayner, "Conditioned Emotional Reactions," *Journal of Experimental Psychology,* 1920, 3, 1–14.

7. A. Bandura and R. Walters, *Social Learning and Personality Development* (New York: Rinehart and Winston, 1963).

8. B. F. Skinner, *The Technology of Teaching* (New York: Appleton-Century Crofts, 1968).

9. Dennis Linn and Matthew Linn, *Healing Life's Hurts* (New York: Paulist Press, 1978).

10. E. C. Tolman, "Cognitive Maps in Rats and Men," *Psychological Review,* 1948, 55, 189–208.

11. J. Bruner, *Toward a Theory of Instruction* (Cambridge: Belknap Press of Harvard Univ. Press, 1966).

12. Robert Johnson, *Inner Work* (San Francisco: Harper San Francisco, 1986).

13. Adapted from Fr. Ray Roh, O.S.B., *Keeping a Spiritual Journal,* Pamphlet No. 80 (Pecos: Dove Publications, 1978).

14. Dietrich Bonhoeffer, *The Cost of Discipleship* (New York: MacMillan, 1961), p. 32.

Epilogue

Additional References to God's Healing for Meditation

After you have worked through the exercises in this book, there may be times when you want additional guidance about how to refocus on your spiritual recovery journey. You may experience the return of an old pain or the surfacing of a new one, or you may wish simply to use different material for meditation and reassurance. We offer, therefore, some additional scriptural references to spiritual healing in these four areas of injury. They are:

> the Lord's Prayer,
> the temptations and passion of Christ, and
> chapters 21 and 22 of the Book of Revelation

The Lord's Prayer

Perhaps the most often used prayer in the Christian faith is the one that Jesus taught to his disciples when they asked him to teach them how to pray. As we look at its structure, we can see that Jesus included a request for God's intervention for injury from experiences of neglect, enmeshment, abuse, and abandonment. To redirect our longings to God, who never changes and gives our lives hope, we can pray this prayer as we make this deepest journey of our heart. The prayer begins with an address and a prayer of worship:

> Our Father who art in Heaven,
> hallowed be Thy name,
> Thy Kingdom come,
> Thy will be done on earth as it is in Heaven.

Then there are four requests in this prayer that seem to match our four deepest yearnings.

> Give us this day our daily bread.

This phrase deals with our yearning for security, perfect care giving, and nurturing: our daily bread, the manna of the desert, fulfills our daily needs, our material needs, meeting the deepest yearning of our hearts. We turn to God daily for this bread, as the Hebrews collected only a day's supply of manna at a time. In this way we learn the faith lesson of "one day at a time," as God nurtures us on our recovery journey.

> And forgive us our trespasses as we forgive those who trespass
> against us.

This phrase deals with the yearning for perfect relationships, for boundaries that are not "trespassed," answering the deepest yearnings of our heart for proper relationships and emotional growth.

> And lead us not into temptation but deliver us from evil.

In the action area of our lives we say, "Save us, oh God. Guide us in the proper use of our power and freedom!" God created our ego, and it is not evil in itself, but the ego is the arena in which we seem to have a naked encounter with the Devil. The agent of consciousness in our psyche, the Light-Bearer, can become infected with a Luciferian pride, which is our exaggerated need to be in control. The poet Milton captured this defiance of ours in his quote of Lucifer: "Better to reign in hell than to serve in heaven."[1]

> For Thine is the Kingdom and the power, and the glory forever.

Most Scripture scholars say that this last phrase was a gloss added to the Lord's prayer, and it has been used liturgically as a completion. It is remarkable that this addition deals with the fourth yearning of our hearts, connection with unchanging divine reality and meaning.

The Temptations of Christ (Matt. 4:1–11)

When Christ was in the desert after his baptism, Satan came to him and tempted him in three areas. It is interesting to note how the temptations parallel the first three basic yearnings we have for connection to and reliance on God. Each one of the temptations of Jesus is not only an invitation to sin, but also an invitation to insanity. When we feel tempted to deny or even abandon our recovery, a meditation on Christ's temptations and responses can be very helpful. The first three temptations seem to address the archetypal yearnings for security (care giving), relationships, and power. But in the fourth area, the yearning for meaning, the diabolic attacks were reserved for the greatest test in Jesus' life: his passion.

Security: The first temptation was one of material security and nurture:

> The tempter approached and said to him, "If you are the Son of God, command these stones to turn into bread." Jesus replied, "Scripture has it: 'Not on bread alone is man to live, but on every utterance that comes from the mouth of God.'"

Jesus is the Word of God. He is "the bread come down from heaven." Our real security, including our physical security, lies in our connection to him.

Relationship: The second temptation was the need to be admired, loved, and accepted without having to deal with real human relationships. Satan tempted Jesus to leap from the pinnacle of the temple. "You can do it easily, Jesus. Just impress people. I could be your P.R. agent; I know how to help you on this. In fact, Scripture itself backs up such presumption. You won't even bruise your foot on a stone." Jesus replies with his own rebuttal from Scripture:

> "You shall not put the Lord your God to the test."

In effect, Jesus says, "No, you don't defy the law of gravity, or you go splat! I choose the limitations of a real human being, of real human relationships. I'll get in line and do the program like everyone else."

Power: The third temptation is about power. Satan said, "All these kingdoms are mine to give to whomever I please," as he showed Jesus all the kingdoms of the world from a high mountain.

> "All these will I bestow on you if you prostrate yourself in homage before me."

Satan almost seems to be saying, "All right, Jesus. Let's not fool ourselves. You have power; why don't you use it for yourself? You can have it all." How often do we hear that in advertisements—the big lie: "You can have it all. Why not?"

> At this, Jesus said to him, "Away with you, Satan! Scripture has it: 'You shall do homage to the Lord your God; him alone shall you adore.'"

Later, Jesus would say, "No man can serve two masters . . . you cannot serve God and the power of money."

Meaninglessness: The temptation in the fourth area—the temptation to meaninglessness, to despair, was recorded at least twice in Christ's passion. First, he was literally abandoned by his closest friends in the Garden of Gethsemane, just at the time when he struggled with his own deepest fears. It is as though the Tempter used this dark moment to challenge Jesus: "Look! Look at your disciples, the work of your ministry! They fall asleep on you; they desert you; and they will even deny you. Your life will have been for nothing, Jesus. It will be like a stick drawn through water. The water will close up and no one will ever know the stick drew a line. Your life is meaningless!" But Jesus summoned all his strength in a bloody sweat and prayed to God, "Not *my* will, Father, but *yours* be done!" (Matt. 26:39 and 42).

Finally, during the crucifixion itself, at the point of death, Jesus cried out with the words of the psalmist, "My God, my God, why have you forsaken me?!" (Psalm 22:2a).

As a human being, Jesus faces the greatest loss possible: his life. All that he has held to, all that he has rejoiced in during his life, is leaving him as the blood leaves his body.

We can connect to Jesus in his desolation when we experience meaninglessness and abandonment. But we can also meditate on the answer to Jesus' anguished cry, the rest of Psalm 22. A theologian, Dr. Bruce Malina, has encouraged Christians to read *all* of Psalm 22, noting that the psalm is actually a prayer of hope in God.[2] This must have been sensed by the followers of Jesus, who were near the cross, and by anyone who knew the Psalms well. After the initial anguished cry and the enumeration of suffering, the psalmist says:

> You who fear the Lord, praise him; . . .
> For he has not spurned or disdained
> the wretched man in his misery.
> Nor did he turn his face away from him,
> but when he cried out to him, he heard him.
> (Psalm 22:24a, 25)

Thus, the psalm itself is the implicit answer to Jesus' intense experience of abandonment and meaninglessness. It asserts that God is close to us in our wretchedness, even when all seems lost. Following the passion comes the resurrection. "If we have been united with him through likeness to his death, so shall we be through a like resurrection" (Rom. 6:5).

Revelation 21 and 22

Revelation 21 and 22 present a picture of the goal of recovery and conversion. In the following section, a commentary on the images from the last two chapters in the Bible, the book of Revelation, we shift to an "eschatological" way of looking at Scripture, a way which describes where we're heading. We begin at the first verse of chapter 21:

> Then I saw new heavens and a new earth. The former heavens and the former earth had passed away, and the sea was no longer.

Remember that water represents the unconscious, so now there is no water. Everything has been made conscious; everything is revealed, just the way Jesus said it would be. So when we reach the goal of our recovery, we become fully, consciously integrated human beings.

> I saw also a new Jerusalem, the holy city, coming down out of heaven from God, beautiful as a bride prepared to meet her husband.

Remember that in the parable of the Good Samaritan, Jerusalem is like our conscious ego, who we think we are in our daily experience. But at the end of our recovery/conversion, Jerusalem has been restored and repaired by God to enter into relationship with something completely fulfilling, as the image of a bride awaiting her wedding day, with all the preparation having been made. So as God has prepared us, all that we are in all our particulars as individuals, God now prepares to embrace directly and passionately.

> I heard a loud voice from the throne cry out: "This is God's dwelling among men. He shall dwell with them and they shall be his people and he shall be their God who is always with them."

This answers the yearning of our heart that God never abandon us. And, second, it is particularly Christian; it is incarnational. When we explored recovery from abandonment in the book of John and discussed the meaning of the term *temple,* we saw that God has chosen to be present to human beings on earth in our very humanity. This passage is a beautiful image of God dwelling among us in our very human personalities—the ultimate contact point.

> He shall wipe away every tear from their eyes and there shall be no more death or mourning, crying out or pain. For the former world has passed away.

This verse offers an answer to our concern about the length of recovery. People groan, and say, "How long is recovery/conversion going to take? All my life? It's so hard, and there's so much pain." Here is a promise that there will be a final state where there is no more death (and all that death means in the change process), or mourning, or crying out, or pain. The whole process that we go through in recovery will in fact come to its term. Then we will see God face to face and have the deepest desires of our hearts met.

> The One who sat on the throne said to me, "See, I make all things new!" Then he said, "Write these matters down, for the words are trustworthy and true!"

This is similar to the time Paul said, "Eye has not seen nor ear heard nor has entered into the mind of man what God has prepared for those who love him!" So Jesus, who is on the throne, says, "I make all things new." *He* does it.

> He went on to say: "These words are already fulfilled. I am the Alpha and the Omega, the Beginning and the End. To anyone who thirsts I will give to drink without cost from the spring of life-giving water.

This refers to our inner yearnings having originated deep within us as the gifts of God, and going toward the purpose for which they have really been designed. God is the beginning and the end of our existence.

In John, chapter 4, where Jesus was speaking to the Samaritan woman, he talked about giving us living water springing up within us. To a Semitic person, water undoubtedly meant life itself. To have water without cost from the spring of life-giving water meant all that we would yearn for in terms of sufficiency would indeed be ours.

Further on in Revelations, chapter 21, John refers to the new Jerusalem. This is remarkable in terms of the imagery of mandala symbolism, of four-part balance and completeness. John, referring to an angel carrying him, writes

> He carried me away in spirit to the top of a very high mountain and showed me the holy city Jerusalem coming down out of heaven from God. It gleamed with the splendor of God. The city had the radiance of a precious jewel that sparkled like a diamond. Its wall, massive and high had twelve gates at which twelve angels were stationed. Twelve names were written on the gates, the names of the twelve tribes of Israel.

Notice how the completion symbol is arranged:

> There were three gates facing east, three north, three south, and three west. The wall of the city had twelve courses of stones as its foundation on which were written the names of the twelve apostles of the Lamb.

The imagery of this magnificent city, which has twelve points of entry, seems to be parallel to the Twelve Steps that are given to us as points of entry to divine reality, points of contact with God. John describes the perfect dimensions of this city, which represents the human individual as God has perfected us through recovery and through conversion. John describes the beauty of the city and all the jewels that are in it. He's in the height of lyrical poetry as he describes God's new creation. Then he goes on to say,

> I saw no temple in the city. The Lord God the Almighty, is the temple—he and the Lamb.

Remember that the temple is the dwelling place of God. Now, because of Jesus' resurrection, the direct encounter with God is not through some human effort of construction, some anthropomorphic point of contact. It's no longer a *place*, but rather as direct a relationship as we could imagine with God; God and the Lamb. So again, our connection point to God is Jesus Christ.

John goes on:

> The city had no need of sun or moon, for the glory of God gave it light, and its lamp was the Lamb.

The glory of God is the light of the city, but the visible light to us in our human experience, the lamp, is again Jesus Christ. He is the intermediate reality that we must have in order to know how to relate to God. But what's so important about our recovery is that Jesus is the human point of contact with God. Once again the fact that we go to God through our humanity is underscored in this imagery.

> The nations shall walk by its light; to it the kings of earth shall bring their treasures. During the day its gates shall never be shut, and there shall be no night.

This meditation closes with chapter 22:1–5:

> The angel then showed me the river of life-giving water, clear as crystal, which issued from the throne of God and of the Lamb and flowed down the middle of the streets. On either side of the river grew the trees of life which produce fruit twelve times a year, once each month; their leaves serve as medicine for the nations. Nothing deserving a curse shall be found there. The throne of God and of the Lamb shall be there, and his servants shall serve him faithfully. They shall see him face to face and bear his name on their foreheads. The night shall be no more. They will need no light from lamps or the sun, for the Lord God shall give them light, and they shall reign forever.

NOTES

1. Milton, *Paradise Lost.*
2. Dr. Bruce Malina, Professor of Theology, Creighton University, "How to Interpret the Bible: A Catholic Perspective," a talk given at St. Austin's Catholic Church, Austin, TX, Oct. 25, 1987.

Appendix A

The Twelve Steps of Alcoholics Anonymous[1]

1. We admitted we were powerless over alcohol—that our lives had become unmanageable.

2. Came to believe that a Power greater than ourselves could restore us to sanity.

3. Made a decision to turn our will and our lives over to the care of God *as we understood Him.*

4. Made a searching and fearless moral inventory of ourselves.

5. Admitted to God, to ourselves, and to another human being the exact nature of our wrongs.

6. Were entirely ready to have God remove all these defects of character.

7. Humbly asked Him to remove our shortcomings.

8. Made a list of persons we had harmed and became willing to make amends to them all.

9. Made direct amends to such people wherever possible, except when to do so would injure them or others.

10. Continued to take personal inventory, and when we were wrong, promptly admitted it.

11. Sought through prayer and meditation to improve our conscious contact with God *as we understood Him,* praying only for knowledge of His will for us and the power to carry that out.

12. Having had a spiritual awakening as a result of these steps, we tried to carry this message to alcoholics, and to practice these principles in all our affairs.

NOTE

1. The Twelve Steps are reprinted with permission of Alcoholics Anonymous World Services, Inc. Permission to reprint the Twelve Steps does not mean that A.A. has reviewed or approved the contents of this publication, nor that A.A. agrees with the views expressed herein. A.A. is a program of recovery from alcoholism. Use of the Twelve Steps in connection with programs and activities which are patterned after A.A., but which address other problems, does not imply otherwise.